山缘

FIRST MOUNTAIN

山缘

Zhang Er

张耳

FROM THE CHINESE BY
Joseph Donahue and Zhang Er

Zephyr Press | Brookline, Mass.

Zephyr Press acknowledges with gratitude the financial support
of the National Endowment for the Arts and the Massachusetts Cultural Council.

Zephyr Press, a non-profit arts and education 501(c)(3) organization,
publishes literary titles that foster a deeper understanding of cultures
and languages. Zephyr Press books are distributed to the trade in the U.S.
and Canada by Consortium Book Sales and Distribution [www.cbsd.com].

Cataloguing-in publication data is available from the Library of Congress.

ZEPHYR PRESS
www.zephyrpress.org

CONTENTS

Dedication of the Original Book:

> *This book is for Grandfather and Grandmother.*
> *This book is for Fifth Uncle.*

FOREWORD   Zhang Er

At some point during our six-year collaboration on the collection 山缘 *Shan Yuan* [Ton San Books, Taipei, 2005], which we are calling here *First Mountain,* Joseph Donahue urged me to write an introduction to the English-language edition. A straightforward account of the sequence of events that triggered the writing of the book, and some basic facts about the geography and culture of China would help, he suggested, Western readers adventurous enough to want to hear my tale.

In November 2001, my extended family in China arranged a special burial ceremony for my paternal grandparents who had died in the past decade, seven years apart, both in their 90s. We, the living, were to move their ashes from Beijing, where they had lived their last twenty-five years, back to their ancestral home in Shanxi province. It was their wish to be buried together in the family cemetery. They had selected a plot and ordered a double-occupancy tomb built when they celebrated their sixtieth birthday. While I knew and loved my grandparents, the world they had come from in rural, pre-revolutionary China was in many ways as distant to me as it was to my co-translator, who has never been to China.

My grandparents had three college-educated sons who lived in different parts of China, away from their ancestral home. Now, as the poems in *First Mountain* depict, they and some of their offspring were traveling back to Shanxi to attend the ceremony. My father, being the eldest son, had supported my grandparents in their old age; his immediate family—that is my mother, my brother and I—physically carried the ashes on the train journey from Beijing to the remote mountainside village of Nan Po, southeast of Shanxi province. Born and raised in Beijing, living most of my adult years in New York City, I had never before set foot in that mountain village in central China where my grandparents had been born, grown up, and married, and where my father was born. And, as I had been raised by ardently secular Communists, it was my first time encountering the rituals and religious beliefs that had shaped those who had shaped my world.

My grandparents also had multiple siblings; some of their offspring inherited the family land and properties and are still living in or around the ancestral home. Arriving and bearing to them two canisters of ashes, I met, also for the first time, the full breadth of my grandfather's and grandmother's family relations. I felt the deep and powerful structure of a Chinese family's *Jiu Zhu* (nine generations and relations) and *Wu Fu* (five funeral garment styles). For the first time in my life I heard the Shanxi dialect in its natural environment, which retains many archaic pronunciations, vocabulary words, striking expressions, and unusual grammatical twists. Although these archaic elements are considered to be the root of modern Chinese, they have largely disappeared from Mandarin, the official version of the Chinese language. I had never had the chance to experience life through the medium of this form of speech. Hearing it made me all the more attentive to everything that was happening around me.

The time for the ceremony is chosen according to the traditional Chinese lunar calendar. The first day of the tenth month is *Song Han Yi*, a day for the traditional sending of winter clothing to the dead: imitations of warmer wardrobes are made by folding colorful sheets of paper, which are meticulously burned in front of the tombs to keep the ancestors properly clothed for the cold weather of the afterworld. The second burial for moving or combining the remains is often set on the day of *Song Han Yi*.

A child of the city, and inheritor of a modern secular worldview, I had never attended a traditional burial ceremony, which consists of several days of carefully choreographed events. First comes the raising of the *Ling Peng*, spirit tent, followed by the ritual invitation of family relations, carried out on foot by the direct male heir of the deceased. Next comes *Nuan Fen*, the warming of the tomb, followed by entertainment for the mourners. We *Shao Ye Zhi*, burn paper money in the evening, and we *Shou Ye*, also keep the vigil at night. This part of the ceremony concludes with *Chu Bin*—a funeral procession of several hundred people, all related by blood or marriage, parading through the village to the family cemetery on a hill outside the village. The tomb is closed after the deceased enters, *Feng Fen*, and a huge bonfire of offerings is sent to the spirits of the deceased on their way to the other world. Mourners march home via a different route, to confuse the spirits of the deceased, and to keep them from following us home. Mourners then eat *Da Zao*, a banquet cooked up in big pots and served in the open air by villagers outside the family. The ceremony then ends with *Yuan Fen*, the making of the tomb perfectly round, and *Fu San*, the returning of mourners to the tomb on the third day after the burial.

The display of offerings to the newly deceased at the funeral ranged from a variety of dishes and bowls of real food, to hundreds of colorful *Zhi Zha*, folded paper constructions such as mountains of gold and silver, palaces, flowers, fruits, animals (sacrificial and spiritual), wreaths, banners with words of praise for the deceased, and paper money for spending in the underworld, printed in denominations of tens of thousands. The real food would eventually be consumed by the mourners. The *Zhi Zha* would be burned to the last bit in front of the closed tomb door.

This burial ceremony, documented in *The Book of Rites*, has its origin in practices dating back to 1000 BCE. The influences of later belief systems such as Taoism and Buddhism were quite evident at my grandparents' burial, though a strain of modernity made a surprise appearance among the bereft—spaghetti westerns and movies about the Russian Revolution replaced the traditional theater performances that used to assuage mourners on the night before the funeral procession. The ceremony I participated in, moreover, was abbreviated in comparison to a full traditional funeral, due in part to the fact that this was a second burial of ashes, and in part to my father's insistence on being prudent and economical. As a Marxist political economist and a devoted Communist party member, he had his reasons.

The experience was more than a cultural shock to me. I was traveling back through time and space to a landscape and soundscape strange yet somehow familiar, where I found my ancestors, my clan members, and an elaboration of the relation of life to death. An entire unfamiliar and ancient belief system was presented to me in the span of just a few days. To be fully alert to all that had happened, and to grasp in the present what it all meant, were the imperatives that spurred the writing and researching for *First Mountain* over the three years following the funeral.

When I was nearing the end of writing the book, Fifth Uncle, whose home I had stayed at for the funeral, unexpectedly died, hit by a passing train behind his house. I was speechless with grief and the book concludes with a deep sense of sorrow for this new loss.

* * *

I have known Joseph Donahue for many years, always admiring the disarmingly easy fluidity of his rich language, and deeply anchored exploration of human situations through time. We collaborated on *Another Kind of Nation: An Anthology of Contemporary Chinese Poetry* [edited by Zhang Er and Chen Dongdong, Talisman House Publishers, 2005] and he was painstakingly thoughtful in rendering the original poems into English. And I enjoyed jostling with him in our often heated but largely humorous verbal matches throughout the different revisions.

When I mentioned *Shan Yuan* to Joe, he was immediately intrigued by the funeral ritual aspect of the project. Not unlike the translation process for *Another Kind of Nation*, we began with a literal transcript from me, accompanied by notations on specific events referred to in the text, and other cultural background. I learned to keep a distance from my own words in Chinese and to recognize the importance of the poetic process between Joe, myself and the book itself. I also learned perfection is unreachable, but humor and persistence go a long way to get close.

Throughout this collaborative version, Joe worked to weave some of the cultural background into the English text. His aim was to minimize the number of footnotes required, and to keep the English-language reader as deeply as possible in the dream of grief and wonder that comprised the experience that the poems attempt to render. The original text has no footnotes. This English version of contains 53 of the original 56 poems. The remaining three poems were published in my previous collection *So Translating Rivers and Cities* [Zephyr, 2007].

I am indebted to Joseph Donahue for his kindred spirit and devotion to poetry.

ON THE TRANSLATION OF FIRST MOUNTAIN
Joseph Donahue

The term translator hardly applies to my role in rendering into English a version of Zhang Er's wonderful suite of poems. It must have been by turns frustrating and amusing for the poet to watch her words wander off into my English. Having no knowledge of the Chinese language and only a slender sense of Chinese poetic tradition, I felt the Chinese poem was both right in front of me, but completely hidden. What I was rendering I could sense but not see. I wanted to get as close to what I imagined was there; but the translation must, whatever the infelicities, sing in English. Long conversations with the poet were crucial. Zhang Er talked me through each poem, answering questions about the text she had provided, about the Chinese version, and perhaps most importantly, about the situation from which the poems arose. The translation, after all, was not only about the words, but about the world in which the words occurred. I often felt my lines were irredeemably vulgar, reducing the poet's nuance and subtlety to crude sense data. I was often quite surprised to find what felt like a fantasia based on failed comprehension met with the poet's approval. Now and then she would say, no that's not it at all, and patiently take me line by line through the poem. When she would mention how a particular image was based on the visual components of a Chinese character, I appreciated anew what I was not able to bring into English. I decided my job was to imagine the poem that was there, both in the English the poet provided and in the Chinese beyond it, and to make a poem in English that honored it.

The working drafts of the poem "Paper Clothes for the Dead," included here in the appendix, shows the way information not immediately evident in the poet's own English rendering of the poem found its way into the final English version. Such came by way of the notes provided by the poet, and through conversation. I did not want the immediacy of the lyric moment broken by the reader's own ignorance, by the necessity to glance at a footnote before proceeding. This was a cultural rather than a linguistic translation. For example, the importation of the term "ritual" to describe what is going on at the poem's start. (A touch of anthropology amid the mourning.) Or, the importation into the text of the historical specificity evoked in footnote 6 on p. 219 (on land reform in the 1950s), so that the reader with only a general sense of modern Chinese history would not be distracted by wondering what time period was being evoked. A further line-by-line comparison of the two versions will make clear to the curious the degree to which throughout the book I betrayed or stayed true to this monumental work.

PRELUDE

1.

Turn on a light.

Illumine my dream

with more than just bright

anticipation . . .

a road branches

a window . . .

mountains hang on the wall

maddening, meticulous

Every tree, a bright thread,

every fold, pure silk

pinch of fingers,

a needle

nonetheless we arrive

sky-high village, centuries old.

In the yards, hundred-year-old voices,
and Chinese scholar trees (Sophora)

a hundred-year-old lotus

        demure as a bride's
                bound feet . . .

Times held to be dead

           return,

but in flames . . .

See, an on-line vagina,
See, internet masturbation
See, severe events and fate await me

blue-grey brick up to sky,

blue-grey stone, paving the yard

long, embroidered sleeves, cambric vest
the trim of the skirt, months of a bride's time . . .

See, a moment, see, a marriage
of seventy years. Is this the light

           of life, is this the sacrament
                that lets you live, that

lets you die?

Watch them, the man and the woman.

Each takes the end of a strip of red satin.

A marriage ritual.

Walking down the slope,
walking up the slope.

Kneel down:

Heaven Earth Ghosts Gods
Father   Mother

Mountain

A mountain to the south
devours the light.

Maddening:

over the bride's eyes,
a red scarf

Blind yourself to the four directions.

Turn around, turn around
only then do you see

in front of the mountain,
the river.

Turn,

you're turning,

the river is flowing

2.

In the banquet room
		of a five star hotel

you say: the trick is
		to push oneself
				into the path of death.

In the first line, let there be
		no possibility of breathing.

Then, write. Then, write until
writing is			to ask for life on a new level:

"The pitch has to be high"

until what is written on the page
		is like what is carved into
				metal and stone . . .

But I have my own idea:
For me, life is simply water,
		as is time, as is poetry,

flowing, spreading.

Shoots break the soil.

a patch of green, a harvest.

You say: "We must destroy
                    all sentimentality in our style."

—And these lyrics of
romantic love?

                    of lilacs, snow,
the Purple Bamboo Pavilion

and the crush of nothingness?

"Transcendental lyricism"
"Intellectual Writing," "Folk Style"
"The Third Way . . ."

          ★

South Slope of Nan Po.
Up early, can't find the way.

Not sure what we're looking for.

Someone awake and up
before us, up ahead of us,

along this river

                    Don't be afraid, go straight up. My wheat field is there . . .

OK, his wheat field is our destination!

Camera, video recorder.
We are crawling on all fours.
How could he ever have hauled

a cropsworth of manure up here?

No trail. Further up, white poplar
                    pines, squirrels, and birds

(the bird's name is Third Month the 6th?

Today is not Third Month the 6th).

Also, now, the low keyed
                    drip, drip drip of
                        a spring, just below us . . .

Later, coming down from the hill,
the sun brushes past us,
past the green, green wheat,

roofs of houses so close
standing shoulder to shoulder

at the foot of the hill,

                    lines of tile

as in a painting of perfect, rational love . . .
of perfect communal happiness

where we would be walking

                arms draped over shoulders

instead I take my hands
out of my pockets
and fold them
behind my back.

Ancestral court yard

all stillness and elongated light.

Motionlessness

        of a hundred years . . .

3.

Grad school days

TACI café

were there other places to go
where you could write a novelette,
read

       dream?

You didn't stay long.
You were smart and beautiful.

Our epoch, you took it in
with your high-end cell phone,

long scarf,
narrow silk skirt
gracefully draping

your slightly
shaking legs—

Life in Hong Kong
        you're drowning in it.
Yet somehow, you feel you

also know about
       life in New York.

You are now prepared, you say,

  to "weigh in" on the

"motherhood

        issue,"

And this is because
you have recently hired
    a maid from the Philippines!

Still, your step-brother,
bewilders us

jailed nine years for joining
    the Chinese Democratic Party

that would be
    a college degree
        plus a doctorate . . .

What type of commitment
    keeps a red guard pushing fifty
        in chronic revolt?

We chat on about

                  family, religion, war,
the impossibility

our generation will ever
get political . . .

Then comes: "What is wrong

with you?

Writing all this
Poetry!

What's it for?
Who even reads it?

You can't make a living with it!
The most you could make is a fire . . .
Why would any
reader want to solve the puzzle
for you?"

—For me? . . .

"Why can't you just
get to the point,

Words are just
a ditch we dig
to direct the flow

of common sense.

say what you have to say, even in a different language.

Oh, gimme a sec," head shaking at
the sound of her cell (Another wrong number!)

Then—touch up her
         make up

"Got to go to a cocktail party

hosted by a reporter

          from the *Times*."

4.

He said: last night
   heavenly light blinded me.
      The beams were like needles

that broke through
the black ice of the night.

So, in his slow and slender words—
It is sublime to regard light as physical volume and
silence too.

She said: the night is
too deep to see light. Doors
are locked, walls are all around us.
No one can overlook their volume.
Silence speaks nothing,
conveys nothing.

           Only when
the eyes of the universe
bleed the purest black
are they sublime.

Ice. Eye. Eyelids
like flower petals
      shot through by

         needles of desire.

Or, to put it another way,
these are simply stars we see
by stepping a few steps
outside the yard. See,
even the brightest
was hidden

by the Chinese Scholar tree

in front of the house of Fifth uncle.

Go further, into the cool
breeze of the field. The stars are
wild and, unlike the predictable moon,

will not be carried home.

(This is no outdoor movie
we must see to the end
if only to keep each other company.)

What we truly admire are,
for the most part, these
erratic rays of light of the

incommensurate afar.

Don't cry, you
tell yourself.

Those who belong to no one,
are wild, like these stars,   wild,
open, moving. Or cry, declare
to the world let all

the helplessness under the roofs
flow from my eyes:
                         heroes   beauties

5.

"Let's grow old together."

How, exactly, will we manage that?

—You didn't say . . .

With phrases no one believes?
With sentences, spun out on a whim?
With the written world, that scratch on a page?
With love that lives in the heart?

The routine we have could
hardly define so grand a word,
love. Wipe the ass, grind the coffee.
Change the diaper, peel an apple.
Shake open the newspaper

and still other exempla
of love's morning:

Yellow in the white of the eye.
Loosening lids, yes, the two
in the mirror
day after day, aging.

Are we really together,
with you in your imagination
and I in mine? Stepping out—
a world where nobody is
lovely, only rushed, unwashed
unbrushed. A crisis? No, not really,

same old same old,

like hand-washing
threadbare underwear—where
is the moisture you felt for the first time there?

"So long, sweetie!
        Have a good day!"

6.

A poem is for you alone.
A poem is for the world.

The world exists so that we might meet.

A leaf pressed in a notebook
makes the forest shed all its leaves.

You wander in and out of
my secret world
thinking only of him.

The blinds are down all day

to keep
that dreamless legend of
splendors and strange events

To speak more plainly,
there were dreams

However, when dreams
became reality,

reality is all that's left.

OK, then, let's skirt this
tangled river of reasoning.

Let's return to what was
before the ancestors.

They walked up the hill.
They walked down the hill.

But there, behind the hill:
Wolves. A virgin forest.

7.

Then you disappear
   into a deep blue
      ink drop on my screen.

No water is too wide
      for me to reach you,

         though here is a river—

No way around it, around it
My path goes straight into the flowing

And here is a thought
    on plum red paper
      dusted with golden powder.

Can't understand it,
    yet you feel it.

      Clear but distant
         as if seen through
           a thin wash of ice

while walking along the river,
chatting about irrelevant things:

    a new job title, relocation, a draft of
    a business memo, an inheritance
    that can't be divided evenly,
    child support . . .

Whatever can be seen is not perfect
like the not perfectly round moon tonight—

Whatever cannot be seen
must already have crossed the river.
The light on the other shore flashes off suddenly.
The party boat carrying music
flows down the river—
                              they are not us

       Blue-green reeds, dew, white as frost.
       The loved one a nymph in the flow of the water

In front of the house,
in summer, the river floods.

Huge boulders roll up over the bank.
People die.

Your name sharp as
              a crust of ice—

              Apricot River.

8.

The four tonalities

are difficult.

They must be voiced

as if singing.

Sound of raindrops falling on a book.

Sha-sha-sha

little frog.

Gua-gua-gua

a far-away snow
stuck to the window pane.

Toothy smile of a tiny sun
swings up and down
between tree branches.

Wings flicker.

Woof-woof.

why always keep the hat on
little lion of blond curls?

"Doggy: *Gou-gou!*"

Deflected tone, correct.
And, the added stress.

"Momma which
letter are you?"

which . . . letter?

My little treasure:

bao-bao, B-AO,

bao, B-AO, bao.

And daddy:

baba, B-A, ba,

B-A ba is B,

the second letter of the alphabet

Ma-ma is more complicated.

M-A, ma, M-A, ma,

in the middle of the mouth but towards the back.

position:

men-two doors walked in and out,
mi-rice, hidden away, can't be finished,
jie-mu-the performance endless
ming-fame can't have,
ming-fate which can't be rid of.

Little treasure

        ride the horse,

ma, gua-da, gua-da, on the ground
ma-yi, ants busy about.

Mom beautiful, *mei*, mom
secretive, *mi-mi*, mom silent,
mo-mo, crow moo-moo, mom
        is also a question mark . . .

The first letter is A
    is love, *ai*
    also is peace and contentment,

an, the most easy and the most difficult

"Where did the cat, *mao-mao*, go?"

The cat was getting old
        and sick.

It is asleep and not waking up.

The cat won't be coming home.

"Where did *mao-mao* go?"

No more.
Dead.

"Where did *mao-mao* go?"

Yes? *Ma-ma* and *mao-mao*
start with the same letter.

"Where did *mao-mao* go?"

9.

Let those in heaven
        bless us

as the dead journey to the west

        on the back of a crane.

At the funeral
        Fifth Uncle points to

a pair of cranes made of white paper,

        sky blue mouths, red crowns, eyes wide-open.

Fifth Uncle is
        a living concatenation

        of old ways

and archaic dialect.

        When he gets going on local history

        it sounds like a stage revival.

He's also a bit deaf.
Whenever I ask a question,
        smiling incomprehension

        creases his face like a dried fruit.

Whatever answers he has
        are the echoes of all
                the desires of the heart . . .

I am finally home.

Fifth Aunt now has a toothache.

But long ago she gave birth
                to a line of cousins.

Wives, husbands,
              sons and grandsons,

living together
    on a family estate

a squared yard for each,
              and high walls.

A whole village
of descendants, not to mention

        chickens, ducks, pigs, cows, goats

           all depend upon protection.

Let those in heaven
                    bless

the bearded and the shaved,

the gold-crowned riding on a black ox

the thorn-crowned riding on a donkey

those flying home on the back of a crane

or the one who floats on a cloud above the desert

those who sit on a lotus

or sit in a small roadside shrine

bless, protect Fifth Uncle's home and farm.

                    *

Delicate devotions tied up in red ribbon.

bless, protect Fifth Uncle's home and farm.

JOURNEY WEST

Xizhi Men Station

As we climb we can almost remember it,

    bu-liao-liao-zhi,
        its unsettling

this rising switchback road

to a train station named for
an immense city gate that no longer exists

everyone's motivation unsettling
in the dimming dusk
yet rushes to get in line,

to jam the narrow entrance
    catch the departing trains

        hey who just cut in front of who . . .

Fair public order blocked outside our car
in the deep chill

Archaic morality
in archaic woolen
undergarments

dispute the interior of
our existence beyond the season.
All climbing the road up to the

modern station

Mother sits on the right
        Father on my left.
                Both look outside.

People, trees planted by people, buildings, streets—
        aesthetics, desires

crisscrossed silhouettes, left behind

and the days . . .

Get up, grind coffee.
Take care of small animals.
Follow the plan, prepare for the day.

You and I do not see the same sun.

Whose sun? So far apart . . .

I finally feel the weight of
        the baggage, the silence.

"Welcome to Beijing"

Wide banner, a toothy snarl.

Travelers, dazed and sleepless.

The waiting room can't decide
        what it should be

and I can't find my Second Uncle.

            Not surprising—

the subtle interplay
        of brows and eyes
                is like a childhood story

                        I never get tired of,
over and above
        any complicated analysis
        of blood relations . . .

It always presses on your heart

                        therefore you don't feel it.
Only these two
        ash filled boxes
                carried by hand

verifiable reminders of

two grandparents,
the cause of our existence. . . .

*

Look up,
the high-rises! And the
slopes and peaks of old-style rooftops,

    all that cultural symbolism

    long since a passing blur
        a pressing, empty weight.

All Aboard

"All Aboard,
                All Aboard . . ."

The moment has arrived
for ID, ticket, fated seat in life, and
feelings that stream away.
What you've found does not fulfill you.
No hairstyle can fashionably
tangle over your eyes.
Yet, what you see is all:

Grey cement stairs
frozen waves of
water and mud
rough, uneven, step
after step, down
"Watch your step!",
(repeatedly cautioned)

Grey rush of tunnels

                currents twisting together.

Is there any pattern to this labyrinth?
You don't want to know.

Seven bags
to visit the relatives!
Where to stow them?

(And the homesickness
untouched for sixty years?)

Mom, Dad, my older brother and me,

(Grandpa, Grandma are both,
admittedly, ash),

all under the same roof again,
(the first time for how many years?)

So close now, knee knocks knee.
A radiator clouds the train's window.
I'm unable to look at you.

The darkness is a silent
platform where no one is left
slowly strolling past,
snug in warm clothes, with
a dog in snow among the trees.

News from New York

Morning is always unexpected.

Caught between
        the awakening of imagination

and last night's dream:
        did I really talk to you?

Emptiness is such a bad connection.

None of your life comes through
your eyes of elsewhere, their
light grey shadow,

 "How's your

      analysis going?"

    —"How's yours?"

No one can say.
Two patients, two

      pathologies.

I put down the phone, as if to
      hang up on you and on
           all the desires you are.

We travel west, we enter
the space that excludes you.

My dream is no longer mine,
            it may not even be yours . . .

Pull the curtain: a small village.
Electric wire poles, a young man on bike,

all fly past.

Over morning's
intercom,
            the day's news:

November 11, 6:30.

A jet goes down in Queens . . .

Meanwhile here as is

the custom even on trains,

everyone gets up for aerobic exercises—

a healthy life is still encouraged!
Although there are no more pastures

or lambs nibbling the grass.

Quick, a call to
New York . . .

the journey west, the journey west

leaving the sun
                        further away, further
you can't imagine my worried look

thinking about you.

This window flies at full speed

a holographic screen
            bright as a fire ball,

as ruins, pieces, explosions.

All is falling once again.

But I would knead the sky and earth
like dough, fleshy
as real as a dream
and toss it to you
back there

where

            there is

no sound—

            New York.

Hou Ma Station Sketch

Two minutes of stillness

Old man, old woman, with
trunks, backpacks, and

once fashionable luggage.

dragging one decade, then another—

At the platform, the train exhales,
leaving behind the bags left and right

A red and green dazzle of

shining things

But let's take our picture
here: the rusted-through train track

a nice post-modern effect—

deterioration, bags or burdens
it happens once in a lifetime

even if you live for another thirty years.

You call out
from a temporary distance
"Quick, switch to the 8:45 train!"

Opportunity is in no rush.
It watches us run, working hard
to fulfill what is required of us at the moment:

the upcoming
underground tunnel,
other platforms to manage.

The traffic light waves us on,
the announcer even seems excited
if not a bit irritated.

"Why bother to run?

The rain will still be
where you're going"
argues the village idiot.

Ahead of us, a field
        the color of the sun.

Unknown, or unrecognized place
A red and green dazzle of

shining things

like new toys. They make

our grief more real.

Hou Ma Station,

what are these feelings?

—Don't want to play anymore?
gather up your seven bags!

A Tunnel through the Heart
of Zhong Tiao Mountain

Deeper into the dark
    as if dropping through the earth.

so lightless and long we feel we are
        pressed upon by the bodiless,

we feel at last we can truly think . . .

Yet, still, we can't make sense of
two simple terms: here, and not here.

All the while counting silently in the dark
on hands and feet, like kids, one second, two seconds . . .

We start doubting our own eyes,
and all that has happened.

Heart hammering, the track rattling,
sounds mingle beneath the mountain.

All light is lost, the wave of the visible
breaks somewhere above us.

Windows are useless. But if we
achieve a certain stillness within us

sitting in this train in the dark

the whole world will pass
through here bit by bit,

the core is
of darkness—

"Let there be light!"

So no one ever sees Him.

On a donkey, along a ridge
is a kind of travel that is different.
What does it matter what you're thinking then—

The dark red silk of the morning
wraps up the small birds.

Were we riding
in Great Uncle's carriage

inside, all can lie down,
the whole family
flesh against flesh
from this hill to that one.

"Niang-niang once took us."

Now here, by ourselves,
and bringing her . . .

Home . . .

where matters of the heart
are burned to ash . . .

How can we believe in mere existence?
Only when blind do we see what we

really desire: to be

Not Here.

One second, two seconds.
Gone, yet more loveable.

I can call his name because of you

A hand burns to touch a hand.

You dissolve into clear bright water

light and shadows
            flowing down.

To believe
is to sit not moving,
is to hold tight

to live and die

and be weightless again.

The only sense of direction in this moment
is deeper into the darkness:

He is on the other side.

Home is on the other side.

INTO THE COUNTRYSIDE

Big Bowl

Routines of solace.

*

Lift up the curtain when entering.

*

On the dinner table, a flowery plastic sheet.

*

Door to home, always open, the papered ceiling always white.

*

Air flowing in through the suspended ceiling.

*

Filling the big bowl, the sustenance.

*

The tally of a family, clear at one glance:

*

Beaten egg, bean curd, shredded meat, black mushrooms, bean noodles.

*

Squatting, Uncle-in-law with bowl.

Laughing, he tells a story.

*

How the Water Conservancy Bureau went about building a high-rise.

*

Eaten from, from the bed room to the living room.

Eaten from, in the bed next to the bed that is next to the sofa.

*

The big bowl is not a symbol.

*

Grandma's mysterious trick: The more you eat, the deeper the bowl.

*

Could you possibly still be hungry?

*

Heaven and earth, linked by a slurp.

*

Eat till you occasionally lift your head.

*

Eat till you see the healing spices of the sun pouring down over all.

*

Aunt-in-law's cotton jacket, with its brilliant flowers.

My Grandmother's Village

Cross the bridge over the hill,
                by the village gate,

                      a massive Chinese scholar tree.

Grey-blue slate road.

Arriving at last at
Grandmother's first home:
The old houses are still there
elder grand-uncle, second grand-uncle's
                         are still there.

Hens, pigs in a pen—

Taking it all in
    brings an unexpected
        touch of grief.

In the living room,
photos of ancestors on the wall.

A desire to trace the cheek bones with a finger
to cup with both hands
the curves of the chin, a petite nose
round moist lips,

to feel the glow of health,
the beauty of a daughter,

as I might feel the clear stream of the Apricot River.

What in all this
could ever be, the true
source of these feelings?

Shall we snap another picture?

Catch one moment
in the thousand years it takes
to bring a couple to the same bed?

No longer quarreling
            about the inheritance

you laugh.

The offspring of a master carpenter
her big hands twist in front of her legs,
She grins and shows her teeth without modesty—

Maybe she senses there is no other chance
to fulfill the obligation of prayer?

Doors closed, window

Flower of double happiness

Wood crossbeam, floor board creak.

Grandma, I hear your cough in my throat.

The shadow of the old family house
left by the sunlight
like her unwilling tears.

meanders
down the hill.

Are you here,
Grandma?

Here, her sadness
becomes my sadness.

Quezhai, your village.

The eternal back and forth
between mountains and rivers—

Can this be brushed aside
without answering?

The Wife of My Elder Second Cousin

Barely through the gate
now, the hill . . .

      *

Her neck-chuff
hangs like a pant leg

with the bulky bag
she has been hefting
for forty years,

the one big-boned among us,
her greetings are so angular

they perk up our
wan faces

staring at me
asking each of us:
                "who's that?"

★

Pines dot the opposite hill.

Far off tree farmers blend

                into white birches.

Not much curvature
                but definitely beautiful

and powerfully, now,

          "who's that?"

    ★

Her son and a daughter
are in middle school—

"Your niece is at top of her class in English!"

    ★

Then: "show your aunt how
good you are!!"

    ★

Daughter with slender body,
delicate long brow, clear bright eyes.

"Isn't your grandpa just like my grandpa?"
Do we really have to be so polite?

Send the old folks happily away
Keep them soothed.

      ★

Her casualness conjures up
ghosts on the tip of
the brow of the sunlight—

I see you. Everywhere is you,
      clear bright golden light
            shining in all directions.

      ★

Her tone, so assured—
I take the measure of my doubt,
from left hand to right,

            weighing . . .

      ★

"Put it down, put it down.
The ashes cannot enter the house.

Ashes can only rest in the spirit tent."

A "spirit tent" is a temporary outdoor hut for mourning,
built specifically for a funeral.

*

"We wear red to ward off evil,
        and drive away the bad luck."

*

Under foot, an exact threshold:
inside the house, and outside the house.

As with life and death, there is
one side, and there is the other side.

*

We breathe in, and,
in the end, we breathe out.

*

With rituals
we cross over, not
quite understanding
or accepting . . .

        (though in Chinese,
        ritual rhymes with reason.)

＊

As if through a forever opened door.
The low stools, the humble, empty-hearted sofa.
They wait for you, wait for you

to believe, and take a seat . . .

＊

(And you, you who
don't know that reason
            is a kind of weakness?)

＊

So is the balky bag.

Raise the Spirit Tent

The ceremonial master
          runs in, runs out,

                    so fast he can't be seen.

Dark-faced elder brother places

the offering dish on the bright altar—

Inside the second spirit tent:

Last night, a windstorm
          the currents of the river
                    tangled with those of the sky.

The spirit tent flew to heaven

                    ahead of time!

          ★

The key
this time is
          nylon string

tied on tight held
          down with stones.

*

Clearly, its best to avoid

    the edges and corners of the wind
    (though to be fair, bad things
      sometimes turn into good things.)

   *

Affairs of a village
go like this:

the same sentence, over and over
      mixed with repeated smiles.

   *

One more time, people
   help us raise the spirit tent!

   *

It's so cold, spring on
Nan mountain arrives frozen.
Get the winter clothes
back out of storage. Get
Ready for even deeper cold.

Little grandson, you
should try on this jacket.

Everybody, find something warm.
Every family has their share
of joy and grief
of coming and going,
wealth and waste
of red moments
and white moments.

★

Now, the roll-call of the present.

Send the magpie to each roof
to call in family and friends.

We have made the sitting room
a circle of tables and chairs.

Call all in, for the ritual
that brought us here
that cannot not
happen . . .

A "white moment" refers to a funeral where individuals wear white
clothing. White is the color of mourning and of death itself; a red
moment refers to joyous celebrations, such as a wedding, graduation
or the New Year's celebration where individuals wear red.

*

Call whoever goes by

        the name of Li

whoever, that is
who is

helping
us in our loss.

   *

Brother Li, Young Uncle Li, Elder Uncle Li
this, sirs, is your ancestor. This one should call you grandma.

Though this is a second burial
this homecoming cannot
           be haphazard

As Grandpa and Grandma
lived their lives so far from home
they cannot be treated carelessly.

We set the ashes in a small coffin

a mattress underneath,
a blanket on top.

Everything is new,
And for those who come to help us

cigarettes and whiskey.

       *

We walk through life and death only once.

We are in this not much like
the waters of the spring that melt,

flow, then freeze again.

       *

Magpie, fly
up hill, down hill.
Call all in. The magpie
calls all in. The
magpie, and
my brother,
and me.

Third Generation Line Up: Number 13

The tally was my suggestion.

(After all, no one else
has my luck, to be born
before fourteen, and
after twelve!)

Imagine this thin paper,
these horizontal lines
could record a real family
history, show all the scenes of life.

Include, as a minor
feminist triumph,
a genealogy
of the women
as well as of men.

Let the true line
appear like a repaired
road on a map.

In traditional family genealogy, daughters are not included in their
family; wives are mentioned by their maiden family name but not
by their own given name. So during our visit, I suggested we should
make a list of all the members of the third generation since Grandpa,
including sons and daughters, first and second cousins and their
spouses, with everyone's full names included.

Delineate the generation.
and find yourself in the middle,
between the shoulders
of two others.

Be this obliging
and unrelated
impromptu chronicler
who sets down
in print

father, and mother
husband, and wife,
daughter and son (they don't belong to you,
the mother.)
Careful, a slip of the pen
cannot be erased.

All relations find
their place

even the dead.

*

The wooden bench in the living room
  welcomes you to sit by the fire.

Warm up your body,
and chat with Fifth Uncle
about things beyond

the cotton curtain,
the dusk and the magpie.

⋆

Ji-ji-zha-zha crying all day,
crying till I have to put on
this blood-stained bridal head scarf.

Till I think of the future,
here on this yellow mud
after the snow.

⋆

Respect, raised up by the offspring
unknowingly, out of confusion,

—our memorial.

Carbon Monoxide Poisoning

What now is—

a foreshadowing . . .

The ultimate conclusion
has been tracking your steps,
even as you rush to save lives.

You don't see   what's ahead.

though duty bound:
"Open the window quickly"
—a perfect Beijing accent
heard early in the morning
in a valley in the mountains
sounds especially rational.

(While a west-bound train
is like a boa biting a heel.
In the corners of the eye, salt crystals.

As if a pair of frozen white moths cried before death,)

Shanxi province is known for its rich coal mines. Houses are
often heated with coal burning stoves in the kitchen. The stove is
connected to traditionally designed thermal walls and platform beds
in another part of the house. During the day, heat from cooking
warms the house. At night, the stove is kept on a low burn to keep
the house warm. However, brick walls and beds are not entirely gas
leak proof, so "coal gas" poisoning is a common occurrence, in spite
of bedroom windows that are often cracked open at night.

I can't remember
how I revived you.

You touched your own face.

        (Icy cold black windows.
           A train passing.)

A car alarm on the street
makes me forget, then remember

Fifth Uncle staggering, eyes red and swollen.

Fifth Aunt, had once again
        taken too many sleeping pills,
           and couldn't get out of bed.

You next to me is not possible
because next to you I have never
tried to dream, have missed
and missed again the chance
to sleep deeply.

        It's already dawn.

The rice porridge is sticky from boiling.

Open the window, eat the mush.

Finish off the leftovers:

        lily flower, bean curd,
            like bits of an old story.

Add a drop of local vinegar:

"I still remember the good times"

        Really? Like when warming
        each other up in blankets
        while burning with a fever so high

            we made no sense, *that* good time?

     ★

Day brightens, time for a walk.

(While the clean cold air washes away
        the poisonous coal gas seeping
            through the heating system.)

     ★

Look, now, along with the sky,
you can see Fifth Uncle along the roof
above us, the white soles of his black shoes

as he treads the emptiness after the harvest.

*

This would be
    a movie's

       final shot:

Grey-white morning blazes brightest

blue

   or

      red

Old Yard

at dusk:

long shadows,
        undesired moods.

We follow Fifth Brother.

     *

Thick wall, high wall, no window,

it would be better to just let go

of our embarrassing nostalgia . . .

     *

In the photo you're alone
corner of the wall, top of the gate,
like faint characters that are carved in stone
                  of our delicate ancestors.

Grey-blue bricks, all the way up.
A two-story building
two entrances
and a double courtyard.

The light darkens.
Darkness spills from the attics.

There's no light left to skim the pages
of your father's well-thumbed preschool book.

*

A giant crop vat under the windowsill.

Yellow corn cobs on a string.

The hope. Year after year
written into plain couplets.

*

no solace in surveying the sprawl of this yard.

*

Darkened light, blinded fire.
Only one family lives here now,
            in the side yard's east wing,

with a name from elsewhere,
certainly not ours.

North wing, locked.
South wing, for the pigs.
West wing, where the sheep sleep.

The yard is paved with brick, and used to dry pine nuts.
The younger generations have all gone off.

They build new houses on the river bank.
You could buy this place for three thousand yuan.
It still has the original single log beam
                    and the carved wood railing.

How much coming and going

            has polished the stairs.

Autumn grasses on the tile roof.

A breeze rustles its teasing whistles.

This was our home

—wanna buy it?

A yard that's one hundred years old
can't handle raining grief

Dirt on shoe heels.

The smear of the memory of here.

You pretend your seriousness is just pretend,
as if only for the moment of
this photograph.

Sweetheart, have you forgotten
How to speak of love
in your mother tongue?

Come, let me kiss
you goodbye, baby.

Please? Before
you go, sweet
heart?

Quickly . . .

THE FUNERAL

Warm the Tomb

The male descendants
brush the dirt into the tomb.

          Each gets three strokes

to gather and intensify

            the virtues of the dead.

The broom has a strip of red cloth.

     *

The female descendants
brush the dirt out of the tomb.

          Each gets three strokes

to take the blessings of the dead
with them in their marriages.

Their broom also has a strip of red cloth.

Red cloth terrifies evil spirits.

The day before the burial, the underground chamber of the tomb
is cleaned and warmed with charcoal fire in a clay pot. Close family
members take part in the intimate ceremony.

★

From how far back has
this broom been handed down?

The broom to establish some kind of symbol

not to stir up questions

This is not some routine tidying up

★

A symbol passes on
Now, with both hands,

We carry a pot of live coals,
and yellow paper

to warm the tomb.

The clay pot and yellow paper are used in the funeral ritual. The clay
pot is a symbol of the living (a versatile utensil used for cooking,
eating, washing and storage of food to sustain life), which will be
dramatically thrown to the ground and smashed into pieces by the
surviving offspring at the beginning of the funeral procession. Yellow
paper is a special kind of unbleached rough paper that sometimes
has prayers or underworld money printed on it. They are burned in
abundance at various stages of the ritual to send money and prayers
to the dead, showing the living's respect for the dead.

*

Let me stay here, and let
the two of you return to life,
        Grandpapa, grandmama.

Who else ever offered me
such happiness, and kept me warm?

Seventy years together.

Haven't you slept together long enough?

Spirit tent, wedding tent.

Now, two grey stone slat biers.

    *

I'm crying.

He turned down the bed

             every night for you.
(Nobody ever tells me about things inside the tent).

Sons and grandsons fill the hall.
        Sons and grandsons fill the hall.

Were you all that happy? You never
held hands, you quarreled and bickered.

Yet there are always string beans
                    and Chinese chives to pick.

Marriage, you said, it's all up to you.
The way you put it

Grandma
made it sound

like fate, like the stars.

The story of your lives
                    is quite fuzzy in places,

               ★

But the end is all too clear.

               ★

Leaves on the poplar tree branches,
clapped like a loud bell.

Swing swing, you held me in your arms.
Sweep sweep, you swept me out the door.

You see I am still dreaming.

            Perhaps about the fox fairy
who rises shining from the chimney.
A bounce, then another bounce,
up over the hill

brightening all the way
down the other side.

Perhaps that fox fairy
you once told me about
now lights up the eternal light
for you, illumines the road
of your departure.

Paper Craft

—Gold Mountain Silver Mountain (with many others)

A moped with a trailer.

A road out of town, into the country.

    ★

These multi-colored hopes for happiness
shine, these handiworks of jubilation
offered to the realm of the dead.

                         Even light up the Yang world:

Celestial peach, celestial flower.

A paper net with purple and white streamers

They remind me of

the wisteria umbra in Beihai park.

They bewilder the youth
(oh, so romantic).

Paper sculptures used in the funeral ritual: flowers, fruits, birds,
houses, banners, wreaths, gold and silver mountains. Banners
are white with calligraphy in black ink; other items are shiny and
brightly-colored. They will be burned during the funeral to be sent
to the dead in their Yin world.

They bewilder the small devils
                    out for mischief

as souls make their way
to the next world.

                *

It's a dangerous road
souls need bright colored scenes

to bamboozle

            the small devils blocking the way.

The souls need flowers like clouds,
                those heavenly fruits covering the land

High, fluttering virtue.

White paper, black characters.

Gold mountain,

                silver mountain,

the palace at the base
                solemn, and eternal

                (not
                a bit like the bungalows
                in the mixed family compound.)

*

Heavenly blue eyed, gold-beaked crane.

Where are you going?
   To harvest stars?
   To cup the moon? To fly
     naked to the naked sun?

Strong wings, paper wings.

  *

What instrument can assess these ashes?

The pen tucked behind the ear
of Elder Brother?

  *

The moped slows.

The sculpted paper is moved into the spirit tent.

  *

Wind, blow over the yellow earth,

   sway the celestial flowers.

(Stick close to me, you
red petals, green leaves.)
An unimaginable happiness
Tortures one who has yet

to compose
a kind of consolation
like the story you told me
when I was young . . .

         ★

The big willow in the yard, cut down.
The apricot tree, cut down.

The grape vine, only a decade old, cut down.

What's left of my rough childhood?

A few hairy caterpillars . . .

Tan-Hua, broad leaved
epiphyllum,
only you persist.
And Grandma, you dreamed of

                two ephemeral blossoms,
concluding that your
grandson and granddaughter
would win a place at

           the university.

★

One night's
ephemeral blossom Tan-Hua
(and now the endless grinding of soy beans)

Neighbors filled the room then
Like now we surround the altar.

Touch here, move things there.
Politely thinking of you, using only good words

remembering

your oracular admonishments.

"Grandma is not going to arrange your marriage"

(gentle click of earrings)

(three-ply sleeves
embroidered trim)

"Look for a home town man."

One who, presumably,
will stick by my side?

All things pass through life and death

like the scent on your cheek.

Like the up, up, down, down,

the hundred and twenty four movements

of shadow boxing,

learned, forgotten, now

                    learned again.

Ritual, Divination, History —

Write them out,
Unfurl them on high

and everywhere

the old, glorifying texts,
the beautiful, glorious words
they flutter, they float in the air . . .

          *

Is it about to snow?

Burning Night Paper

Can
Love recall,
      can Love

         remember itself?

What
time is it? Is
this the moment?

Stay up,
keep your vigil
through the night, stay up,
keep the hours, keep the memory, snow.

Thread, thread, thread,
entwine and tie and tangle me.

Spindle, this is the night
one thinks of the spindle, of
a glossy black long braid, of an oil lamp,
of a daughter-in-law
rushing to weave

Several times during the night before the burial, stacks of yellow
paper are burned for the dead in the spirit tent. A candle, or
nowadays an electrical light, is kept on throughout the night
as well. Family members take turns keeping the vigil.

red cloth

for herself before
her in-laws get up.

The deeper realms
                    are hidden in the

overlapping maze
                    of warp and woof.

Love never wants to go back
except in a dream, which is now,

a pinch of tonight,
a volume of darkness, of light

of an ash-red
bandana,

burning.

What desires to be said?
What desires to be written down?
Burning,
burning down,
so we can leisurely converse
so the full story can be told. Slowly.
Burning
one stack, another stack.

You no longer try to comb through the thread in front of you.

Is it time?

Entering
the third watch,
the vigil, deep in the night.

Night,
can it remember,
can it be remembered?

Like night itself, the embrace of the fire
flickers into every orifice.

Caress
the tended flame
blazing with fulfillment —

We stand up,
we kneel down.

Night,
can it remember,
can it be remembered?

red ash.

Gift List

On pink paper
in delicate, small, script:

raw paper	five stacks
fire crackers	one thousand
canned fruit	one can
steamed treats	eight rolls
food for spirits	eight dishes
treasure mountains	a pair
flower banners	a pair

birthdays, weddings
        funerals

              the gifts are

gifts . . .

Zhang family, Li family,
next time the other side
will go through this

an event like this.

Check the list
make sure you're not

scrimping or exceeding.

Go in, go up stairs, write down

what you have brought

        that's on the gift list,

then: kneel down before the dead.

With the obligations
properly noted,

take heart in knowing
grief has an exact dimension,
a size, a weight . . .

Drop for drop
tear for tear, wet nose,
wet eyes, fresh, cool and fair

            the true measure
                    of a particular life?

Underfoot, yellow, frozen earth.

Up stairs, down stairs,

Accept it, I said,

the steps of villagers
        as they come and go

as respects are paid
honestly, if not kindly

What I want to say is,

you should step into this world
and take a look:

the hill is not high, quite round,
rough with pines and white poplars,

river not too deep, wading bridge
one step high, one step low

(sheen of icy branches
caked with coal ash)

Note what else happens—
for example, how the topic of

9/11 upsets everyone.

How the Phoenix satellite TV channel from Hong Kong
dwells on the air tragedy in Queens,

emotional, yet measured.

Inches, and one tenth of an inch,

measured much like the
illustrations in this,

death's textbook:

Pink horses in the yard.

My snotty grandnephew (!)
in baggy cotton pants,
full-faced and wet,
              kisses me pink.

fragrant candles   a pair
black cloth   one square
red cloth   one square
steamed treat   one roll

Paper Clothes for the Dead

It is sooooo

        cooooooooold . . .

Take out
       coats, gloves, sweaters

From the luggage, put on all the shirts,

Elder Brother's woolen long johns, on loan

It's the first day of

         the tenth lunar month.

We wear them all, insulated jackets,
insulated pants, hats, shoes . . .

as we begin to make
winter clothes for the dead

(paper shirts, paper pants, colorful coats)

You sit right outside our circle,
under the flourescent light

your face darkens.

It is sooooo

coooooooold,

your skeleton is trembling.

Watch us perform
our ritual craft.

Last year's old felt hat,
trim loose and curved up,
buttons on the front of the jacket,
lost, black cotton jacket, the batting
exposed where I can't mend it.

My sister-in law says,
"Weren't there any good clothes?"

Your great grandfather and great grandmother
were buried in old clothes, in rags.

The hat now in the casket
—carried, now, out from
the cave at the foot of the hill—

came off your Fifth Uncle's head.

The old yard was confiscated
by Mao. Your grandparents lost
the house, and farm and animals.
They had to dig a cave in the side of a hill,
put a door in it, and call it home.

Have you seen it?
Now it is a storage room.

Even in this new house,
with its heating and hot water,
my hands are still cold.

How could any hole
in this earth not be cold?

Scissor the clothes, brighten
their color, approximate
some new fashion style:

hat, suit, tie, otherwise
the neck will be cold—
your neck, landlord,
landlady, mine.

Cave dwellings are commonly found along the Yellow River in Shanxi
and other Chinese northern provinces. A semicircular column is dug
into a thick layer of sediment in a hill and windows and doors are
added to seal off the front opening. Inside, the dirt walls and ceiling can
be paneled with wood or bricks or left as they are. Although the cave
can be made quite comfortable (there are modern hotels built in this
way to attract tourists), it is generally considered to be a dwelling for
poorer individuals. My great-grandparents suffered a great deal after
the communists took over and were treated most harshly during the
Cultural Revolution, when they were driven from their home into a
hillside cave. I once visited their cave: it was extremely bare, just a hole
in a hill by the side of the road, with a single door but no windows.

Fifth Uncle says,
your great grandpa himself
opened the sheep pen
to the Revolution
waved his hand,

     OK, he said,

let it all be divided up.

Even their mattress and blankets
were taken from them—

Learn to live on loss

The family motto
written on a scroll on the wall
of the formal sitting room
of the old property.

Your great grandparent's house
was crucial to the underground
in the fight against Japan.

Your great grandparents snuck food to the
Anti-Japanese Association.

The day before
the Japanese army attacked,
your great grandparents opened up
the family larder,
they called people from
miles around to help
themselves.

All that night the
farm animals were agitated and
at daybreak they bolted into the mountains.

The Japanese marching along
the Apricot River
dared not climb the hill.
They got nothing!

That is one part of
           our immense pride.

After the war, in the fifties,
some villages revolted against
the landlords,
even killed a few.
But in our village, it was
our great grandpa himself
(the village head
for many years)
who called the people
and divided up his own property.

Even today,
Elder Brother says,
our family has many members.
Many live too far away
but others come to help.
Of course we treat them well:
we don't scrimp on liquor
cigarettes, candy and cookies,
we give many gifts for
a day's labor.

It is soooooo

coooooooold

but less so with all of us, somehow, related.

Building the outdoor fire pits for the feast.

Cooking, setting the table

Carrying the coffins,

Holding the funeral banners,
wreathes, setting off firecrackers,
filling in the grave.

Whatever we are doing now
we are reliant on each other,
are blessed by, are ensured by,
the virtues of the dead.

Cut, cut with scissors, red hat,
yellow boots, sky-blue tie, apricot,
yellow scarves. Only such colors
honor where the ancestors now live,
a celestial heavenly palace,
an underground palace . . .

a gold mountain,
a silver mountain.

Ancestor Tablet

I heard
this tablet is a fake.
The real one was smashed in the Cultural Revolution,
thrown into the Apricot River.
Now it's a step
in a wading bridge.

The words once on it
are gone, long gone, erosion,
water, sun, moon.

Later on,
under Deng Xiaoping
the tablet was exhumed. But the
smashed bits did not fit.

The original?
Even when my grandfather
was a child
it couldn't be read clearly.
The characters gave
only hints:

The stone tablet was located near the family burial ground, not far
from where the old village is located, with row after row of names
carved onto it. Each row represents a generation of male offspring
whose given names share a common character.

The Carry That Load Generation,
The Heaven Generation
The Emblematical Generation,
The Great Generation,
The Masonic Generation,
The More or Less Able Generation
The Been Here and Gone Generation . . .
And here are the Most Prosperous
the Brightest, the Lights from

five hundred years ago,

when a Truth married a daughter of a King

inheriting mountain and water,

farm and garden,

gaining official position,
(how high is Xing-ting's office?)
joining the army, went to study to become a Juren
went to the capital's Guo-zi Jian
as a student, the name, Jian-hou
or Ke-guan (Can-Be-Made-Presentable),
or Ke-pei (Can-Be-Cultivated) (a good name)
or Ke-wen (Can-Be-Warmed-Up),
or Ke-run (Can-Get-Moistened),
Ke-yun (Can-Be-A-Nice-Cloud),
Ke-liang (Can-Be-Of-Virtue)
so poetic. A farmer was called
Hong-ren (Grand-Duty),

Or Hong-yin (Grand-Office-Seal)
or Tai-hui (Supreme-Emblem),
or Yuan-hui (Original-Emblem)
or Tian-ding (Heavenly-Ritual-Vessel),
is that a bit over the top?

Perhaps it's only
the wishful thinking
of parents, the fruit of
their boundless ego?

Again and again
the graveyard gets
                    relocated.

Leave those faraway pillars,
Leave this tablet erected by a son
of the fifth generation, in the Qing dynasty,
(that student in the capital, Jian-hou)

For the last hundred years,
no entry appears on the tablet.
What happened?

China Shanxi Qin-shui county
Long-gang town
Liang district
Nan-po village
Where is the record
of what did not happen?

The memory of the living
is empty and blank.

North King middle district,
Number Ten Li family ancestor
Li Zhen, Zhen Li, a Truth
None of it looks real,
like any kind of
persistent attempt at a past.
But my effort is real:
look now,
one stroke after another
writing it out till my hand hurts.
Warm breath on fingers.

The crops all hauled in
empty ground empty

On top of the head
early morning
blue and green
                    —for no reason

offspring:

A Truth
or not
I can't see you.

Seal the Tomb

I

To the end, in the end,
one torch, one unified fire

a transit to another world
in a singular burning.

One must cry, out loud now,
or else be mute in the next life.

Offspring in mourning, bent at the waist,
leaning on the Cane of Lost Cries,

undyed sackcloth, gunny clothes,
Zhong-Shan suit, Mao suit,

one road, walking along, walking along,
one road, crying, crying all the way.

Set off the firecrackers,

set off the firecrackers

at the moment of going away.

Hold up the banner, the wreath
in a multi-colored procession out of the gate;
drive away the ghost,

shy away from the evil,
avoid the evil . . .
sputter of explosions
pop, pop, pop, pop, pop . . .
down one road, walking into the dark,
towards your underground chamber.

One torch throbbing with fire.
No time left to drift away into the ceiling mural.
Let us meet again, amid some rendition
of the human disaster
dragging wings of fire
and destroying everything.

Later, we can spread the scientific ideal
that says   whatever is   can be known.

These souvenirs of space travel,

       tickets for an underground train.

"Even the seats

       are in flames"

"Sorry, I didn't say goodbye when I left"

Out of a door, through a gate . . .

Collar and buttons must all burn clean

Only fire can understand the customs of another world:

celestial flowers, celestial fruit,

        gold mountain,
            silver mountain

Light up the palaces
of our memory, only burned
clean can our longing be carried away.
Cry, sob within your heart
ten thousand times,
but let no tear fall from your face.
Tears can't be carried away.
A teardrop on a coffin
can't be carried away.

The name of this town
Waters of the Heart.

Dirt hill, home.

The zip code here is

048200

II

Push open the tomb door.

The blue stone door creaks
with what else but the

           endlessness of past events.

Little golden coffin, little red coffin.

Live to ninety nine, sweet honey,
and keep looking at me, your
gaze will dry up my tears.
Separate and far apart,
such tender distances—

flesh next to flesh,
breathe in, breathe out.
There is nothing
that can separate us. In
this world why cling
to an ill-fated perfection?
What is a thousand years?
What is the cause for love, and
What is the knack of never showing love?

Do you have any wisdom about this?

A marriage of seventy years,
dare we say it was passionate?

Or was it only these ashes
in my cupped hand,
no longer divisible.
I bury you, you bury me.
Lie down, I am here.
I am here—

As a sailor might say,
our relationship was over
the minute you left that hotel room.

As the Buddha might say,
                there is no room,
                        and there is no you.

And since there is no you,
I bury myself.

Yellow
    dirt covering
        yellow
            dirt . . .

III

We often have a certain

   curiosity

      about people who are

           not awake, not awake:
who breathe in, breathe out,

and remain alive   in between . . .

But not awake
       what kind of feeling,
          of sensation, reaches us?

Awake, having awakened,
one has to face certain matters.

"What should we have for dinner?"

"Are you gonna get the kid, or should I?"

Routines keeps us breathing.

They constitute a philosophy of

constant erasure and revision.

What real reason is there

to bind bare threads from

tender garments

that can no longer be worn?

Only ritual.

Lie down, sleep, dream of
a giant white rabbit,
a pair of red foxes.

You said, not believing
is the real death of ritual.

Speak out loud. Say something.

—the sun silently swallow the tears of the North.

Speak out. Say something.

                    Do you still love?

Cry noisily. Cry noiselessly.
Feel free to say what you feel.

By now, they are walking far away
and can't hear us.

Dream of goldfish.

This is the last time.

IV

"Pears
can't be sent
to a loved one,

apparently,

        unless you
want to appear
to be, as you are,

             pared."

Send a lover
pears
to pair, for
pairing.

for health
for clearing the air,
even the air in the lungs,

a pear to cool the secret fires

a pear or not a pear,

a pair or to pare,

my question.

*

Pare, parings, leavings,
leave the tomb door closed

there is only one way to go,

the death road

and everyone
will walk down it.

*

People on a hill,

    a hill of people

        a hill full of people.

*

The family must block the road back to life, light up
the flower wreathes, flower banners,

        gold mountain,
           silver mountain

either a gash in the ground
or a heavenly palace,

burn the paper clothes, the
paper hats,

fire, a warm muzzle
in the dirt hole
in front of the tomb.

Breathe, breathe in and out,
as the fire crackles.

Breathe, fuel the
turning, fleshy body
the souls left alive to walk
to die, to die
as if to be born
could ever be a choice.

★

Kin buries kin
a shovelful at a time
one scoop after the other
so I bury you, and
curse, and say this with hate:
one shovel, two shovels, three shovels,
the handle done up in red,
go away ghosts, souls
don't ever come back here.
Leave our bodies to our own lives.

*

In the end, we even
shovel dirt into the air,
and then we seal the tomb.

The underground ceiling,
is lit by the firecrackers.
Scare off the spooks, fire.

Time is only for the real.

Silks, thin threads, all burned.

Cancel all of it, even the credit card
—the number got stolen
while sending pears.

Leave, spirits,
we do not want you.
Don't follow me home.
We throw dirt into the air.
We don't see you.
We don't look at you.
Don't ever return!

*

The living are now
returning to the village.
They take care to take a road
the dead don't know.

V

This long procession is
a northeaster of
flowers and banners.
No ritual is ever fully described,
certainly not this ritual
with all its gaudy splendor,
firecrackers, taped music,
outdoor movies
shown in a place once home to
a truly religious theatricality.
It's all hot and noisy, for your sake,
in your name, for death's sake,
under death's name.

Seen from
where you are now,
what does all this
amount to, a few last
mementos of a senseless,
and inexplicable world?

Is color, for you,
just black and white? Or is
a ball of fire a lively eternal light?
Was Heraclitus right?
The river rolls relentlessly
past the graveyard on the shady slope.

This dream's mood could be called

                      creamy turquoise,

or glittering green pine stone,

or peacock blue . . .

Wave pushes wave.

Let it be here,

           the end.

You smell nothing,
therefore you believe.

Mint   pine sap

in the wind, in the cold, in the sunlight.

You don't believe,
           therefore you see

a sacred scarab.

And over there,

a red wheel barrow

ROUND THE TOMB: RETURN ON THE THIRD

Winter Solstice

So nice,
the dreamy winter
—how can such weak light
reach into obscure
matters?

Blue sky,
red roof top,
dazzling wall
so bright they blind.

Only the pines
keep their needles.
A white sedan

                waits at a light

looking down from a window
all becomes mine
for
a moment

then
all starts again
the car dashes to where
it should go

the flying dust
is beautiful,
a present for me—

that can't be held.

Like the sky, the wind
the mood . . .

    ⋆

My daughter is
singing

"Ashes, ashes
we all fall down!"

New Year's Resolution

Merrily,   merrily,

        merrily   merrily

life is
    but a dream . . .

My daughter
sings, bobbing head
waving hands
        inadvertently
            strokes the heartstrings

you and yours
me and mine

we look at each other
        from our separate boats—

sunlight
on your hair

sunlight in my eyes
rolling. "You are still laughing!"
what else is there, really,
except laughter

except
this one moment
each looking
      at each other

row,
row, row . . .

gently . . . gently . . .

At the Intersection

A difficult problem. The red light
   is a subset of

     the not-red light.

But what order of
operations
   is at work?

Afternoon traffic jam:
   a tangle on both sides
     of the equal sign.

Glimpsed in the
traffic, a deep, full smile,
   the single-most brilliant
   numerator of
     the entire

afternoon,
   which is darkening.
A truck begins to back up.

The warning
beep, the looming
   rectangle
a massive shadow

not quite

that winged lightness

    that can't be further reduced

        perched on the electric wire

Best would be
to leave all this empty.

Not even a single car is here.
Let the crossroads itself

be bare,

just a perpendicular axis

no longer
the guilty cross

remembering the careless afternoon
when we became
children

Clinical Bedside Trial Protocol

Here is the heaven of
   clear results:
   all is black or white,
not pearl grey or cloudy blue.
One binder, then another:
  the eternal record
of human life's
simplest attributes:
    height, weight, age, pulse,
    blood pressure, respiration rate

liberated from any name—

File 1, File 2, File 3 . . .
Inclusion criteria, exclusion criteria.
One notation, then another,
required to be in
black ink.

You say poetry is
   like that, a force
      flowing into the heart.

Let's take note.
Lets sleep awhile
and see what
flows into the heart.

Who really knows what
    floods me or you, what details,
what meticulous

    pornography

Gold

At the
train station you

said thank
you, just

    like that,

        kissed me

like the

        sunlight does,

just like
that

dis-
appeared
into the crowd,

just like
that

gone
a presentation
    now incomplete,

just like
that

on the street
the sunlight was
                pure gold

    but she, the gold

doesn't believe
in anything—

the sun
the gold train
pulls away

we're formal,
    we're difficult

(to the
most loved,
the greatest
pain)

remember the gold,
    not the rain or wind

write letters
about

forgotten fashions
and dim sum

as if, were the past real,
    the future would be also.

Even when gold is
stolen is it ever really lost?

The train stops.
Doors open.
Travelers in, out
no him, no her

fate is
like gold,
it's that simple.

Two Brides

Many years have passed.
I can recognize your bones:
    bleached face   thin like my
husband, bleached face
     helping me
buy the train ticket,
     saying I've changed,
     leading me   into a grand hall
        is this an occasion for celebration?
It seems to be   my wedding (?!)
     A voice shouts: "Make-up!"
A leopard skin bag
    is placed on my head
       as if it were a hat
(if this is to be
    carried on my shoulder
       shouldn't it fit   a bit better?)
"Lights! camera!"
Dazzle of ceiling light
(you are still the director)
then we see   a bride in white
ringed by a crowd   and you
you stand next to me
you   and you and you
I don't recognize   you
I don't recognize

      the bright window of morning

New Year

In the end life has been   pretty good
       today is the
              new year.

What happened   last year?

We met, loved,
wrote
many poems,
observed a few rivers.

There's no going back.

   Not everything matters.

Right from the beginning
   we should have wept

when our hair, lips, fingers
felt happy for so long
              and we laughed loud.

(Yes, joy should be shared.
But why necessarily
with you?)

No doubt this
year will be
    the same,
a   good time.

How can we endure it?

A New Research Project

This is not
a new research project
    but a dream, a Japanese steak house
    on Miami Beach—what year?
with whom? Or was it
the Yan-An hotel
    in Shanghai?

Where else can we live
except in poetry,
gathering, there, like travelers?
All relations are a crossroad,
a bewildering knot,
a complication
in a plot:

How does time pass?
Day after day,
a stream flowing in curves dislodges a pebble,
cracking open one's own head.
A flower falls.
An army retreats,
disconsolate, after
you've gone.

Who is that?
The red skirt
            under the moon
pouring its imagination down on
a pair of blue jeans
or the petals of the rose,

quickly flying and floating
to manage with moonlight
the matter afterward—

What is that? Heartache
falling across a page
as an ivory-colored elephant
serenely steps on
these fine skeletons.

(How can blood be summarized?)

Last night I ran after the train.
In hand, a wooden trunk,
locked with an antique locket.
I have no place to put it down.
I don't even know
                  where I am,
      except   a big wooden trunk.

You see me, call my name,
            you come help,
pale and thin, full Manchu
(like my current husband).

You bring me fresh flowers
still as shy as
you ever were.

The hidden thoughts
of these days are bright.
They shine: sunlight, moonlight.
River, please pluck me out
of
    these romantic
        entanglements!

Let It Go

How can one
conscientiously
give up consciousness,
     and then even   comprehension?

For example, that patch of orange
stirs memories and
associations, explicit
yet inexplicable:

soft comforter, mom's ear lobe,
blond hair, a taxi cab—

Whatever should be done
in the mind is already done,
including adopting a cat,
and subsequently
the possibility
of getting run
over right out front.

The shrink says
to clutch, to not give up,
is really a disease, an addiction
fed by the pharmacy
of childhood. She said so
because she has been trained
and paid to say so.

As for you,

first you said:
expect nothing.

Then you said, wait.

But there is
a contradiction in this
that makes a certain pair of stars

shine all night long.

Right at this moment
the telephone rings,
yet there is no voice,

no sound coming
either through the wires

or through the magnetic field
underneath the ground that would

complete the interaction

between overlapping
materialities.

So, tell me how
to render it, how
to let it go,
put the sadness down

and give up the plan to step in front of
a speeding car. Put the weight down. Yours.

That has nothing
to do with the stars,
nothing to do with you.

Jack

My life is
unrelated to yours,

it's that simple,

like two freak tails
weighing down a tadpole
in a macabre
drawing

or a balloon
flying off into the sky.

In water or in air,
the two may not be equally

conducive
to living.

What do these
two patches of the dark
knots of broken lines depict?

Maybe these are legs

that haven't learned how to walk?
Imagined wings?

"This is Jack! He angry!"

Beauty is the only
                    true chance event.

Others, such as Jack
are like two glass balls
on a girl's hair band
thrown away
by a boy hanging
on bare tree branches,
this moment's
metaphor

where blue,
can't be explained
out of the blue.

"Jack, Jack" the little girl
walks along and cries out.

Woodpeckers fly east or west
or maybe it is

a peacock flying southeast

Could one of us
still be angry?

The boat disappears
                    in a translucent mist . . .

The Eastern Han dynasty (25–220 CE) ballad "A peacock flies southeast," tells the tragic story of Madam Liu, who was rejected by her mother-in-law. Despite her husband's protestations, her mother-in-law succeeded in sending her back to her parents' home. Liu's family pressed her to remarry a high-ranking official. Madam Liu pretended to agree and then committed suicide at her wedding by jumping into a pond. When her former husband heard the news he hanged himself in a tree in his family yard. Their families buried them together in the same tomb. The poem has 357 lines and is one of the most well-known early narrative poetry works in Chinese.

Monday Café

Full of longing,
I walk into a café.

Flowered shirts
are all round
though springtime
is still locked away
in the subway tunnels.

I sit down, turn away,
    but can't elude
      the day, the
morning news.
It's the day
you and I so
often met. Monday,
what have you
come to tell
me now?

Other stories of
love's blossoming
under such quiet glances,
amid the flowery patterns
of life, under sunlight,
gathered up, and
scattered and not
in accordance
with my hope?

I am waiting, only
not able to
acknowledge this fact—
yet I am not waiting for you,
or the future, to walk up
and smile at me.
"It's better
we not
communicate,"
you said, which
let you disregard
the breathing blossoms
their rising and falling

and the coffee,
cold in the cup.

People tacitly agree to be
healthy and outgoing.
    They clap excitedly for
    whatever performance
is on the screen.

So then:
after knifing and
    forking through
    the heart's fill
of dessert, and my
expectation
on the plate
already evolving
into a wound

hard
to look at.

(Is there any
beauty that can't simply be

"comprehended?")

Leather Jacket Ad

Wants to tell you
the secret of everyone—
the charming smile, the exact
gesture, the right
expression.

Everything is
under control,
foot light, side light,
the foundation powder
put on just now
guarantees you pass through years
that have basically been deleted from the picture.
Is the interior lifelike,

the over-layered, irregularly
pulsing
internal organs?
Take a shower, put on
a richly-scented leather jacket,
put on pearls, shining and sleek
so that even you fail
to recognize the
true self.
See, the jacket
pleases   everyone.
Kick up a storm,
lower your head,

consider certain
hidden parts of the body.

Then, almost carelessly,
let the edge of the
          jacket fall back.
But showing just a bit too much
is enough to make you call out
stop, afraid no one wants
to see such details.

Of course it may be best
to shrink back into
the old showbiz fakery,
to seem to complete
your runway stroll
utterly fulfilled.

Though perhaps what
we long for is less like
a fashion show
and more like bio class or

an autopsy, with stomach
and heart and lung that can be
compared to the gills
of tropical fish.

The fashion's water
      world is full of

         bubbles, surfaces.

Run the ad once more:
Walk bravely through hailstorm
and keep warm in that leather

a violence against the body
too remote to remember
at the moment

Ivy Vine

Green, green to the waist, deep,
sharp, guard your feet, your legs, pick up
a leaf, press it down, on the page,
trace the unavoidable
triangle. I am one of the
angles, I don't belong to you,
(I don't belong to *you* either)
yet I can't be torn off.
We could just call it
        an entanglement:

fishy, stinky, smeared
over a whole face, adhering
to the hand, joyfully, gently
stroke, not fast, not slow.
We could just call it
maturity: the sun passes
between our thighs, we chat
about the spring's
balsams and azalea,
learning how to live, only
then can we withdraw
and not bat an eyelash,
leave a stretch of empty field
and distraught roses.
Then, if we've "got the balls,"
we'll wear tea-colored sunglasses
filter time and light

proportionally and so
control the expression and
the tone of the picture frame.

This is his art, you expertly nod your head.

You passively become
the background of the world

where we would be
carefree, paying no price
except perhaps solitude,

as if *have*, and
as if *not*
follow us
all our lives.

Yesterday Afternoon on the Hudson

Premonition:
A rooftop maze
    where I smoke.

It's raining,
it's not,
     the rain

falls only into the river.
Some unknown boat,
long and wide drifting

downstream.

The boat's draft,

    is surprising,

as might be

the flash of

    a killer whale

or what's below

    the deck of
      an aircraft carrier.

The boat a barge
     low in the water
     hauling steel beams.

The spine of
a black fish in the
shape of a mountain

gently rising and falling.

When I'm about to turn away—
little white sails, two
flags of hope
flutter toward the
top of the mountain,
closer, closer still
on the Hudson, upstream

a sailboat

    a white carp

thin   almost bodiless

a vision lost in water
and wind

motion as
gentle as a dancer
in the full-length mirror

fragrant sweats

a rhythm of steps

or is it the rain?

Aren't you excited
for this possible
moment?

No, don't
turn around,
you have no time.

Can this be called victory?

Leave the real-world
vessels behind,

Let this flower of   a mood
link the directions
that can't be unified.

Hold tight with both hands
the flower's hip

Move against each

Cry out loud.

As if this rain
could render you
free . . .

It Doesn't Matter, Darling

Blue sky,

       white cloud,

many roof tops

               endless stories
                  goings-on in the windows

Don't stand there like a stump
Don't leave anything behind,
             carry them all away

need nothing,
         use nothing

             can't see, can't hear

Eyes red, ears close to the ground,

the lawn, the playground,
   children kick off shoes
      and jump in the sand box.

Blue kickball
skidding around.

The overhead helicopter
                    comments on the traffic.

Fly, freedom,
before you are lost.

In the end
Isolation and grief
          will be precious

like shoes stepped into
     without noticing.

Bend to pick up a child

          bend a thousand times,
                    in a thousand ways

and be born out of a pure seduction.

Locked in the embrace of each other, don't turn back

          You will double the weight, you will crash.

And yet broken apart,
there is nothing.

Sing a song while
washing the vegetables . . .

          This field is a bog, I can't lift my feet.

—Twist your way out, no one cares.

The carton is empty,

     I smell my own funk.

Holding the child,
     what can't be endured?

A train passes without sounding its horn.

Balloons and sticky soap bubbles,
          (none are dreams.)

"Goodnight." "Goodnight,"
I say it to you every night.

"Mom, mom, look
the bunny has escaped!"

Darling, it doesn't matter.

Dusk

is hard to avoid when

        we're still far from the dream.

What should be cried over, has been.

No smiles to be found,
only dusk, bringing with it

the moist call of the rain

a moment neither quick nor slow

and as for the tea cake,
look, but don't touch.

I would make a flower
arrangement on your body

gulp down ice cream

honey drips down
to be licked up

a bull dog bites
it doesn't let go

pink tongue maybe

only noodles
in your bowl,

miao, a cry disappears,

        tail being wrapped by a boa.

Day fades into night

a pot of Indian tea

can I guess what's on your mind

a color never yet seen

you wrote about black ice
the volume of light
and of silence

banners and markers
around a construction pit

flap quick as a flirtatious eye

you're only interested in
"change," and appetite,

     a plump strawberry pie

     shuffles past in delicate steps

        leading away the lunch salad . . .

Does this count as "change?"

strawberry, after all, is really
the truest color and the
taste of all women
(more rose than rose).

Flowers can be
complexly arranged

      when the point is
           to attract a bee,

to offer homage to love

or do the flowering stalk
themselves aspire
      to self-perfection

these vases of
rainy dusk can't run dry
the first drench of autumn
patiently cleans the street

then the news hour

many "major developments" . . .

you, too, must know
our dialogue
is so primitive
utilizing no words,

it almost never involves
current events
therefore is
mostly
like the dusk
that can't be
avoided
even if

we wanted to.

It's Raining

It's pouring
the little girl wears a hat
pointy straw props up the sky
an old man is snoring once again

No that's the thunder that fades away
the rain entices, slides down the French window
and pools on the ground

a little sad, like
tears or days
without leave to

escape from printed words

Step out into the
bubbling puddle
the way a fairy might
walk across a cloud—

A flag is waving, blue
like black, white like grey,
red like the memory of a mood
or the twitch of a fish tail
in a grocery basket.
In that flopping
is the entire weight
of wanting more life.

Without the hat
that hides the flowing hair
that would bring down a kingdom
you might sink into the water on the marble sidewalk
that is becoming a lake
without depth yet
somehow it catches
both
passersby
and blurred hopes
which can't be abandoned.
What do you see? What do you forget?
What does it mean, this sudden depth of feeling?

Strange and stranger animals
are appearing in
Wonderland's lake of tears,
but you don't change.
You are neither bigger nor smaller.
There is one road, it seems, and
you walk it to the end
because you are a man.
Women change their minds
this way, that way
yet they always like to
spin around the same spot
flip the water from their hair
then go home.

This rain is an
answer to last night's dream:
you lay on my desk, called my name.
"I am sick . . ." you said.

Then I heard
the cough, the rain
si-si-so-so, the ripple
and whisper of
clothes, stripped off,
tossed on the bed, wet.

Home. The rain
stops, time to go.

Tiger Woman

Shifting from one
plane of reality to another
you leap over the table,

sit down robed in tiger's skin
all while on a mobile phone.

Can poetry keep pace
with your imagined
companion in the woods?
Whether for a long
life together
or a short fling,
at the moment
you're not choosy.

Back home is the world of landlines
and answering machines
empty and silent
as desire in springtime

slush in the street
slops over

There is an old Chinese legend about a hunter who meets a beautiful
woman in the forest and marries her. She bears him several children.
Then one day she jumps out of the window, turns into a tigress and
disappears into the forest.

romance with all its
fatal and obvious cruelty.

And so the delicate
thorn of the imagination
dipped in drizzling rain
is sharpened into
a gleaming tiger claw.

Through the wall drifts
a Buddhist prayer chant.

Eight commandments,
or is it ten, someone is
singing the dharma.
You may chose not to listen,
but you still have to hear it.
The chanters walk away.
You, too, are only passing through.

So then, leave this black tavern
at the edge of the

mountain before you

served up
in dumplings.

These days, you can
talk about video games,
cut your hair
short like a boy, keep

your natural feet, or
acquire tiny ones,
traditionally bound
as you quickly walk,
force a smile, feel refreshed,
lightly touch up your brows,
then jump in front
of a train . . .

(oh wait, that's
another story!)

Do you know why
Anna Karenina did that?

"Mom, you are not smart!"

Hope you will be
smarter than me.
On this sheet of white paper
where everything can be written,
write nothing. Emptiness
is spreading; silence
bares the fangs
I am unable to avoid.

Obviously you are passing through.
Still in a red shirt,
still not buttoned up
in line for the evening party,
not talking. We are always not talking

only looking, and other organs
not just our eyes are
shifting positions.

This glass of cold water
gets me drunk.

I will pretend to fall in love
tonight. Show off my animal nature.
Write down all the entanglements
that will embarrass me
tomorrow morning.
Man, woman,
as long as you are not choosy
there will always be

some tail.

Parallelism

We
can continue
to write like this

we can continue
to live like this—

holding our daughter
as she draws a crow
on my notebook:

as Hu Shi might
have noted

one butterfly flies to the sky,

        one butterfly suddenly returns . . .

We don't need to practice
how to grow old, how
to shuffle through
one mode of verse
then another.

The quote is from the first modern Chinese poem written
by Dr. Hu Shi in the 1920s in New York City.

What did
SiKong Tu recite,
his hands folded behind him?
The FengYan Song had been sung.
Also the Water Long Tune,
all those old forms.

We don't know if there
was parallelism
back then but
those old poets
followed this basic rule:
eat, eat, drink, drink.

In this they are
our contemporaries.

What will give you a taste of
the essentials of life?

A substance not too thin,
not too thick, not raw,
not overcooked,
what else but
a perfectly rendered
                    poetic mode.

In the turning curve
of the river, write down:
"I have traveled here."

SiKong Tu (837–908 CE) was a poet and critic in the
Tang dynasty who demonstrated 24 modes of poetry.

Then, like the monkey king,
proceed to pee at the spot.
"Live between
reality and distance"
(this bewilders me)

      the distance of reality,
         the distance of things,

at the sky's edge
at the lip of the sea
the distance
between water and water.
The Yangtze and the Hudson
flow together, together
therefore flows
all distances . . .

      It is easier for me.

But, is it harder
for the living,
or for the dead? Is it
harder for the one
loved, or the one hated?
Is it harder at home,
or travelling?
Is it harder to be
a man, or a woman?
To be you or I?

And so we
write . . .

Return on the Third Day

Who will hear this?
If you don't cry now
in the next life
you'll be mute; cry out loud
and without tears, do you have this skill?

Raise the incense overhead,
raise it three times. Show respect
three times, at every mound of every tomb.

Show respect three times,
turn around, burn paper again.

Fire warms whom?
Whoever dares to seriously
receive this truest flame?

Only the ones who have left.

On the photograph
your grandparents smile.
Great grandfather does not smile,
in his torn felt hat, black cotton jacket
                    batting spilling out—

and your great-great-grandfather
has no photo from where
the ancient dead look at us.

Closely follow Elder Brother.

We take off our hats and bow
beneath our bundles of suspicion.

Mountain god, earth god,
Do we bow to all four directions?
Do we repeat one, repeat two, repeat three
hundreds thousands of
time's reincarnations?

Who presides here?

Who is pleased, and who is angry?
"The world belongs to you,"
Chairman Mao remarked.
So, it belongs to us?
Is life a kind of luxury
or a chewed-over crust?

        Eyes are burning, body explodes
        I can't see you. Where?

(Dante)
In the middle of the journey
of our life
I came to myself
in a dark wood
where the straight way
was lost
[Nel mezzo del cammin di nostra vita
mi ritroval per una selva oscura
che la diritta via era smarrita]

Not hell, shadows
or savage dogs. But the
fire is real, consuming my heart.

Can I now speak with you,
send you my regards
from among the living?

Bright smoke of yellow paper

steam from a plate of buns,

rising over our heads. Pay your respects
to Heaven   to Earth   to Ghost   to Divinities

to here—

　　　this is for you, Big Guy
　　　for you.

And for myself, for all still alive.
Kneel down, kneel down inside
the heart space
in front of you,

　　　your sunglasses

the outside scene of hills
sunglasses shade the face.

Suck the shameless root

pine groves lush between the legs

Neither an expression of
eternal love,
                or hope for fertile soil

not symbolizing anything

it's just fishy and sweet
lick, lick again. Therefore it is
meaningless?

Can this
give us life and yet
be meaningless?

Ancestors   father   mother

middle age, astray in middle age

(Qu Yuan)

For these are what I cherish
you could kill me nine times
                I'd still not regret it

One of the first documented Chinese poets who lived in 300 BCE;
poetry prior to this was written anonymously. The two lines are
extracted from his *Li Sao* (The Lament).

It can also be a way of saying:

>   take me, take home
>   this offering
>   burns

The message that would be
one sheet of paper
is too insignificant to be
mentioned in the field of late autumn
where one string of blue smoke
burns like longing
lingers only a few steps away,
unsent
in the morning sun. Would it be
better to mail it home using
a non-standard address:
as one would send
a big gift package of
strawberries and chocolates and pears?

Will you be there to sign for it?

This is yet another place
that offers us no answers.

So what? Where else can we go
to escape from human desire?

In this unsettledness
without a pain or an itch
pine branches nod their head

affirming the map
covered in morning dew.

Wade through the river, step
over this shovelful of dirt,
west bound.
On the coffin lid,
the Taiji,
seven stars that form
a big question mark, is that
simply the traditional décor?

Though practiced for generations
these rituals seem too rough and ready,
too crude, how can
this really be
a legitimate belief system?

Grandfather, you lived to ninety-nine.
You said, you had twenty years
to ponder death
yet you forgot to tell me
the secret way out,
the hidden way, up hill,
down hill?

Blow lightly, breeze
bearing the scent of life

Maybe the mystery is living—
As death is woven into a flower basket
                    and placed on the altar:

I am making peace
with myself, catching my breath
after masturbating
to a photograph
voice . . . nudity . . . you,
melting.

My hand smells like a wet dog

the scent of sunrise
shall I ask you?

WU TAI MOUNTAIN

East Passenger Train Stati

Again, from here,
a journey, the way
more clear, more logical
than it seemed to me as a child.

Over the phone, we agree to
               meet

Xiao Lin, Shu Cai, Li Jun and Mo Fei.

At ten past eight
        at the entrance

The 103 bus arrives.
Grandpa and grandma
emerge from the station,
up one stair, down another,
in their arms, slung
from their shoulders
in packs on their backs,
are bamboo baskets
        giant wooden
           basins, small
             bamboo chairs,

pickled mustard-head,

Xiao Lin, Shu Cai, Li Jun and Mo Fei
are the names of my travelling companions.

sauce
　　two nights,
　　days train ride

Chengdu
　　to Beijing.

Grandpa and grandma
loved me. You, only you,
somehow can refuse me.
Sit down, stand, even if
you say nothing
it's a kind of hint,
it leaves a kind of track:
I am looking across the crowd,
yet I can't find you.

I tried all my life
to forget about you,
then I turn around and
see you squeeze
through the surge
your smile overflowing—
"Can I take you home?"

Or "let's take the road,"
　　　　so happy . . .

　　　You are dreaming

Now
not dreaming:
torrential pedestrians,
        tidal bodies, drops
            from my forehead

on the journal article
in my hands,

I'm standing next to
the clock tower of fashion
fretting I'll miss the gist
yet unafraid to catch
the wrong train.

Quick pages.
Subjects change,
new themes, as if
out of
nowhere,
as if I were to
search the east by looking west—

Xiao Lin (little grove)! Shu Cai (tree talent)!

Splice them together
        a magazine spread
            devoted to subtropical lushness,
(how many trees
do those names conceal?)

Mofei Mofei (what if, what if)

He is worried, is jumping
around like a monkey

Our guide Li Jun, who
has gone to Hong Kong,
what advice has she left us?

"Be careful on the road."

Departure is in
                    35 minutes.

Wu Tai Mountain,
            Wu Tai Mountain.

We eat yellow cucumbers.

And, in the summer,

                        cool melons.

Wu Tai Mountain or Five-Plateau Mountain in Shanxi is one of
China's major Buddhist sites. Hundreds of temples there attract
large gatherings of Buddhist monks and devoted worshipers.

Slow, Slowly

The blade
skims the fruit
(was it an apple or pear?)

brightly colored peel,
the drifting fragrance
compels attention.

It should know better
              than to settle here—

seeing that apparent
tranquility, demands a type
of control
as does anger.

The phone rings.
What you are looking for
is not me. Open the backpack,
crack the curtain. The sky
is getting dark.

Outside, on the departure platform,
the sky is irrationally
waiting.

The train doesn't move.
We are what is moving,
like in the movies,

this way, that,
bend waist, raise head
with great effort hoist

the overstuffed bag to the overhead rack

all the time shot through by
a glare so bright
that we are turning
transparent and
self-consciously solemn.

What should
happen would happen
but the opposite is true, too,
and neither has any relation
to any divinity, and none
of this necessarily
corresponds to your
imagination.

What can be
borne up must not be
all that burdensome

and as a result

the contours of the body
are exhibited more precisely.

*

The train doesn't depart.
The platform stays where it is:

*

Now, are you still missing me in the fine drizzle?

This flower sticking out from the side is too bright,
crowding, occupying a place
one shouldn't, it's criminal,
the way all longings are.

No, the way all memories are.

This moment is
transparent, like a leaf
dripping wet, outside the window.

So cut it off. All you need are scissors.

You are an expert in cutting flowers.
You love to arrange them,
but you're not so good
getting them to open.

The following program
of course will be followed.
Before the character steps out
the stage must be darkened.

Clear your thoughts, clear
your throat, take a shower,
change your clothes, you might also
consider changing the sheets.

Ready your heart and mind.

Only then can you, like last time,
risk everything for
a sweet taste.

A bear after honey.

          ★

Slow, slowly come.

          ★

The train doesn't depart,
intentionally, or not intentionally

watching

you stand there
pissing with some
difficulty
slow, slowly

Shave, put on body powder.
Throw on an undershirt, a turtle neck.
Check the ticket, clip the ticket,
turn it in for the metal tag for the sleepers
then when you get off the train
you redeem the ticket.

(It's as if nothing has happened.)

We stay where we are.

Has time even passed?
Is this the same platform

              or one just like it?

The train is still not departing

tormenting

Secret Words

You book the same room
            as if you'd planned it

as if the room were a theater
            for you to show me some big dream.

We have been through way
too much together

countless events

engraved in our bones and hearts.

We can't feel peaceful
or even talk to each other.

Drink tea, break open seeds,

Eat peach, watermelon, talk about life,
earlier ones, the current one, the
future one which is also

the secret words of a poem,

of a puzzle, a maze,

you hold in your hand
my answer, the one way out.

Therefore we are thrown
into companionship on the road.

Climb aboard. Climb the mountain.
Cast off the boat. When sharing
a cabin we only tell stories, write poetry, and
draw sketches. *Count your blessings*
Count my blessings

with me

with you all

share the warmth of indoors,
the opportunities that
require not just

the hundred years of
fate that lead to marriage.

You want more?

How about flowers
perfume
water
incense
food
lights

gifts to the Buddha.

You can't get enough of
             my white, smooth shoulder,

the whole top half of a woman's body

where the last traces of sexiness
             can still be seen.

Other fresh flowers drift downwards
longing to meet the cool seagulls

and hunting dogs

but here, alas, they turn into

crows, ducks, pheasants, trees,

draft beer of the Southern Plateau

and a big vegetable stew.

Off-color jokes
walk out of the cool shades of
             the Purple Bamboo Pavilion.

They pounce on endangered poplar leaves the size of a palm.
We've known each other—
ten years, a hundred years,
             quite a while.

*

You follow the teachings

yet still can't distinguish those
                wild flowers in your heart,

their names, their looks, even when they appear

as photos in the evening paper.

Curve your arms to form an O: too perfect.

A flower in the mirror,

                            a moon in the water,

a blurred emptiness
                    a lighted trap
where the turnip can't be pulled out.

Yet even this dream has
a night when its finally done.

For example, tonight.

You say I say I love you,

do you believe it or not,
                or is this just, for you,
                        a poetic tongue twister?

Roundness is not
necessarily fulfillment

but a slippery smoothness of

perfumed body cream

not necessarily a protective circle
for example   this wedding band

this hamster wheel of iron wire

this exercise for its spirit

*

this humiliating mix of water and mess.

Cleaved, bloody,
        all have to die.

The mountain sees you
        standing next to me

        doing your thing.

An image boils in my heart.

Does she wear a bra?

Is this soul baring
        or porn?

Why do the strings of rain
incline to you? This bloody mess
is cut open for you to see,

while she still sits on the opposite bed,
watches me, lights a cigarette.

I would prefer not to
believe such an ending:

rain drops wrinkle the water

ugly water slowly opens its mouth

           ★

Progress
lights a stick of incense—
some water, some green cleansing
blooms at the waist line,

a spice pocket
a stone staircase,
a robe, wide pants.

Buddhist nuns hand in hand

walk a long way.

They don't beg for coins or cry,
they hold hands through the noisy town.

The unknown go to another's home.

There is no "alternate edition."

The scrolls have closed their door.
Pour out these waters, give voice.
No line is meaningless.

Gather up the liberated
depth and density
of this summer.

*

Meditate in the coolness.
Impenetrable long sleeves, prayer beads,
life and death flow through all.

Sitting with your legs folded up is like spinning the web of desire,

a cool pavilion at the waist of the hill.

Wind blows, sweat stops.

The lower half of the body feels cold.

You would like to walk to the very edge,
climb to the mountain top,
examine this rough and severe

endlessly
turning wheel.

Want to eat something? A banana?

Professional smile of a photographer.

The grammar of the sentence cleverly controls
                          the intensity of emotions.

Sensitivity trembles, has doe ears

pastel-colored at the root,
a grove of trees waits a hundred years,

a thousand years, patiently.

The grove of trees watches a butterfly in the wind.

A mouthful to the east, a mouthful to the west,
alert to both beauty and nutrition

the butterfly flies up, flies down

is suddenly reborn in the hand of a poplar branch.

                *

Say this is wisdom, though
not as sound as, say, the naïve white
of a pagoda's shaded by floating clouds.

Try not to blur the solemn décor and the principle of the pearl beads.
Try not to pull your clothes off in erotic abandon.
Don't force yourself to step off the lion or the lotus seat.

This cannot yet be construed as our virtue.
True reason is a tangle of vague teachings.
We talk because it is difficult to talk.

Eternal light of a Buddhist lamp.

Celebrated banners, high above.

Only when the head is reverentially covered
will dreams dare to design an end to silent burning:

Outside the door, a sky full of stars

Hear the indigo-blue secret words.

The Death of Fifth Uncle

Certainly it was their fault . . .

Travel west, now, on the crane's back—
what were you thinking
                        that last moment?
                        at day break

was there fog,
        was there rain?
Or was that the wind
        that made the sound of
                        flowing water?

Last night: a huge drum, an opera on TV.
Does Fourth Son visit his Mother, Fifth Uncle?

The shoes sewn by Fifth Aunt
slip quietly across railroad ties.

Emptiness between the iron rails.

So close below, so far away.

Past or future sounds,
brazen as your brand-new Mao jacket.

Yet on the morning

of the tragedy

heavy dew in the new spring.

Overdose of blood pressure meds.

Drunk on coal gas,
nearly deaf.

Fate is a hole in
emptiness

Can't see, can't hear
eyes red, ears pressed to the ground

All the wailing can't explain
a pile atop the cut stones,
blood, flesh, clothes
dragged along the track

turned into slush

turned into water.

The shoes
Fifth Aunt sewed   for you,

how did it begin?
What was its name?
In death, where is it?

There is only a train
that doesn't blow its horn.

Fifth Uncle, did you catch wind of yourself?
Didn't you feel your feet in the shoes?

Certainly it's my fault.

        Fated, as I am, to
            "bring bad luck to men."

      *

From behind other men
No
when I say no I mean no. friends for a while

I don't want to destroy you,
even if you possess the air of
a fence beside the rails

or, transparent and patient
you wait for me to adjust

the rhythm and elasticity in the middle of the sleepers
because we forever meet in the summer

grow close in the crisis or the sense of crisis

our arms already possess the strength of the two rails

not too far not too close
desiring

sweating profusely—
do I want your life,
or
       just the opposite.
the sense of measure just right, with good training
therefore can hold tight

modern medicine says

press down with full force
       one inch above his belly button

one, two, three, four, five

use both hands

one a fist, the other, spread open

(hand gestures, of course, are full of proverbial meaning
and are immediate, no need to second guess.)

He vomits out the bitter soup
made long ago inside his mother's womb.

              Soup of tea, liquor, coffee,
                     and the heartfelt stories told

         at the dining room table.

*

Therefore
everyone's a lover. human love. lust.
overstep the rail, breach the rail,

after the affair, flee.
You don't believe it happened?

if you don't
just look at me, brilliantly colorful,

like the sun just rising above the horizon—

Sunrise is a body covered with scars,
with knife marks, with gunshot wounds,

the scars on the head of a monk.

And these compose our inner map of

the underground where the engines run on desires.

Flesh touched is the ultimate surface, only . . .

The good part is too.

Darling.

Though flesh turns into

slush

turns into water

driving wind   rushing thunder

there is none

Should we not use
the imperative?

Blue or red?

Could we turn around
And eat again last night's porridge?
Could I never have walked into your yard,
sat on your bed, seen you walk cross the roof?

Protect and bless spirits,

Fifth Uncle's home and farm.

The sky after autumn harvest is also at fault.

Turkey Seeds

Energy   Function

    Message

shape the habits of the heart.

Liquid seed,

                granular seed

seeds inherited, newly cultivated,

what Buddhists would call

the seeds of sudden enlightenment,

"meat pie falls from the sky, etc."

                    (a free lunch!)

Everything can be a seed.

And so the Thanksgiving turkey.
And so, unclean as we are,
            we must be seeds, too?

Floating in the sea wind

floating in the flow of the sound

the tide of garbage

Junk of our forbearers.

Other's junk, that of those
                    just ahead of us.

Lately I've been stirring
time and space into a bowl of corn meal
to feed, in the dark shed,

wide open eyes
                    the turkey.

Then, plucking the feathers,
I slip a needle into a dead breast
and shoot salt water and pure vegetable oil.

Broiled now, ready to eat,
to add to the chemicals we are,

our meat a mixture of medicine and additives.

Born in a hospital,
        as most of us are,

there is no choice of
returning to a life in the fields.

There is no forest, not even a grove.

Perhaps I should put it more positively,
After all, we've already walked out,

walked out towards the world.

Thus, at one end of the dinner table,

I watch the gulls of the heart
scan the seas outside the window,

wide open eyes, plunging for fish.

Maybe they can carry off in their claws the
nuclear-powered submarine hidden from our eyes!

The submarine is no symbol
passing in and out, in and out of

a deep water Pacific port.

Misty fine drizzles.   A bit cold.

How you set the table
depends on how you conceive of it.

Plastic pine tree, little pine cone, silver foil, snowflakes.

A knife falls, hand to floor.
Will there be uninvited guests?

Measuring cup, frying pan,
big bowl, small bowl, finely cut spices,

olive oil, cooking wine, long apron.

One cut, two cuts of meat.

Torque the pepper, sift the salt.

Bind into a bundle, with a string, the already marinated veal.
Use the pipette to measure all you want.

The sauces are bottomless:

cream, soy, lemon.

Various cheeses, delicious scent.

Should I add crushed ice?

The oil is hot, the fire is right,
into the pot it all goes!

We sate and stew
ourselves
in this world

pi-pi-pa-pa

A DUET
Zhang Er & Joseph Donahue
on Translating *First Mountain*

Chinese Original (from 《山缘》，唐山出版社， 2005):

送 寒 衣

冷呵，大衣，手套，毛衣和
行李里所有的衬衫，甚至
大哥的毛裤，（阴历）十月一
都穿上了。棉衣，棉裤
帽子，鞋，老去的人穿新衣
纸衣，纸裤，五彩的外套
你就坐在我们圈外，荧光灯下
脸色发黑，冷呵，骨架打抖
看着我们手工；去年的旧毡帽
卷了毛边，前襟的扣子
掉了，黑布袄。绽棉花
够不着也缝不着。

大嫂说，
哪有好衣裳？
你祖爷，祖奶奶穿着
旧衣服下葬，帽子还是
你五叔头上摘的。从窑洞里
抬出来，祖爷祖奶就住山根
那孔窑。老院没收了
地主，地主婆自己挖窑。去看了？
现在成了储藏室。新盖的房，暖气
热水，手还冻呢。土窑哪能不冷？

铰吧，铰，换个鲜艳的颜色，新款式：
压舌帽，西服，领带，不然脖子冷——
你的脖子，地主的，地主婆，我的。

五叔说，
你老爷爷自己打开羊圈
挥挥手，分就分了吧
家里的铺盖也搬出来——
"学吃亏"的条幅悬在老院正屋中堂。
打日本，你老爷老奶家里
住游击队，捐粮给西盟会。
日军要扫荡，头天把家里粮库
打开，方圆几十里的乡亲都喊来分粮
一夜牲口闹得不睡。逃难
天一亮，往山里钻，日本人顺着杏水走
不敢爬山。什么也没捞着。
这就是我们家的传统。土改
别的村斗地主，闹出人命。
咱村，都是你祖爷自己（他是多年的老村长）
喊人来分财。

大哥说，就是今天
咱家人口多，外面的人多
事也多，人家来帮忙，咱就厚待
人家：酒是好的，烟是好的
糖果好，还的礼也比得上人家
一天的功夫。这么冷的天
都沾亲呢。大灶，烹调，摆席
抬材，打幡，花圈，放鞭，填土

都靠众人，托祖宗的福。
铰呀铰，红帽，黄靴，天蓝
领带，杏黄围巾。才配得上
老人住的天宫，地宫
金山和银山。

Sending Winter Clothing[1]   First Version (7/22/2008)

It is cooold/cooold[2], out coat, gloves, wool sweater and
all the shirts in the luggage, even
elder brother's wool long johns, (lunar) first day of the tenth month
wear them all. Cotton filled jacket, cotton filled pants
hat, shoes, the died wear new clothes
paper shirt, paper pants, colorful coat
You sit right outside our circle, under the florescent light
face darken, cooold, skeleton trembles
watch us handcraft; last year's old felt wool hat
trim loose and curved up, buttons on the front of the jacket
lost, black cotton jacket, cotton filling exposed
can't reach (you), can't sew (for you) either.

Elder sister-in-law says,
where can there be good clothes?
Your great grandpa, great grandma worn
old clothing when buried, even hat
was picked off your Fifth Uncle's head. Carried out
from the cave[3], the one at the foot of
the hill. The old yard was confiscated
landlord, landlady went to dig the cave themselves. Have you visited?
Now it is a storage room. This new house, hot air
hot water, hands are still frozen/cold. Can dirt cave not be cold?
cut, cut with scissors, change to a brighter color, new fashion style:
beak hat, western style suit, tie, otherwise the neck will be cold—
your neck, landlord, landlady, mine.

Fifth Uncle says,
your great grandpa himself opened the sheep pan
waved his hand, OK, let them be divided/confiscated
even the mattress and blankets were dragged/carried out—
"Learn to Eat the loss/accept the unfair treatment"[4], the scroll hanged

in middle wall[5] of the formal sitting room of the old yard.
Fight the Japanese/Anti-Japanese war, your great grandpa grandma's house
lived the troop of guerrilla, (they) donated food to Ximeng Hui/Shanxi
    Anti-Japanese Association.
The Japanese army was coming for raid, the day before, (they) opened up
the family food storage, called for village people 10 miles around to come
    to take the crops
all night long, farm animals agitated/unresting can't sleep. Evacuation
at day break, into the mountains we went, The Japanese marched along
    the Apricot River
dare not to climb the hill. They got nothing.
That is our family tradition. Land Reform[6]
other villages struggle against landlords, even killed a few.
Our village, it was your great grandpa himself (he was the village head
    for many years)
calling people to divide up his own property.

Elder Brother says, even today
our family has lots mouths/heads, many live outside
events many, others come to help, we of course treat them
thick/well: liquor is good (quality), cigarettes are good
candid and cookies are good, pay back gifts also match up
their whole day's labor. It is so cold
all are related (by a bit). Big stoves/fire pits[7], cooking, setting the table
carrying the coffins, holding the funeral banners, wreathes, setting off
    firecrackers, filling in the dirt
all rely on everyone, blessed by/ensured by our ancestors' virtue.

Cut, cut with scissors, red hat, yellow boots, sky blue
tie, apricot yellow scarf/orange scarf. Only these (color)
can match where the dead ancestors live, the celestial heavenly palace,
    earth/underground palace
gold mountain and silver mountain.

218

Zhang Er's Notes to Joseph, 2008:

1. Sending winter clothing is a traditional occasion that happens on the 1st day of the 10th moon, when the living send miniature paper clothing to dead ancestors. Paper money and food offerings, including paper clothing, are set out in front of the ancestor's tomb; incense is burned, prayers are offered, paper money and paper clothing are set on fire and burn to ashes as a way of "sending them" to another world. This is also the time to transfer bones/ashes or move tombs.

2. the original has an expressive word "ah", after cold.

3. Cave dwellings are commonly found along the Yellow River in Shanxi and other Chinese northern provinces. A semicircular column is dug into a thick layer of sediment in a hill and windows and doors are added to seal off the front opening. Inside, the dirt walls and ceiling can be paneled with wood or bricks or left as they are. Although the cave can be made quite comfortable (there are modern hotels built in this way to attract tourists), it is generally considered to be a dwelling for poorer individuals. My great grandparents suffered a great deal after the communists took over and were treated most harshly during the Cultural Revolution, when they were driven from their home into a hillside cave. I once visited their cave: it was extremely bare; just a hole in the hill on a roadside with no windows and a single door. *Yao dong* literally means a cave hole/cave dwelling.

4. *Chi-kui*, literally, "eat the loss", refers to a deficit, usually in money. To accept unfair treatment.

5. *Zhong-tang*, literally, middle of the hall, the wall facing the entrance door of the house. The entrance room is usually used as the family's formal sitting room, with a mantel (usually a table) in the middle, with chairs arranged symmetrically on both sides. Above the mantel is the *Zhong-tang*.

6. In the 1950s after the communists took over.

7. Whenever there are big events in the village, people build outdoor fire pits to cook with giant pots and pans for hundreds. Eating is part of any village event, be it a birthday, wedding or funeral. *Da Zao* literally means a large cook stove.

Second Version by JD with ZE's comments (2/3/2011)

Paper Clothes for the Dead[1]

It is sooooo

coooooooooold . . .

, Take out coat, gloves, sweaters
and put on all the shirts in the luggage,
even elder brother's woolen long johns,
It's the first day of the tenth lunar month.
We wear them all, insulated jackets,
insulated pants, hats, shoes . . .

Then we make
winter clothes for the dead

make here,
sending is later
when we burn
them.

Paper shirt, paper pants, colorful coats
You sit right outside our circle,
under the florescent light

your face darkens,

it is sooooo

coooooooold,

your skeleton trembles.

Watch us perform
our ritual craft.

Last year's old felt hat,
Trim, loose and curved up,
buttons on the front of the jacket,
lost, black cotton jacket, the batting exposed
where I can't , can't mend it.

My elder sister-in-law says,
Aren't there any good clothes?

Your great grandpa, great grandma
were buried in rags, old clothes
the hat in the casket was directly
from your Fifth Uncle's
head.

Carried, now, out from
the cave at the foot of the hill.
The old yard was "liberated"
 (in the land reform)Your grandparents lost
their house, farm, animals,
had to dig a cave in the side of a hill,
put a door in it, and call it home.
Have you seen it yet?
Now it is a storage room.

there was only one hat
for the family. Fifth
uncle gave his hat to
dead. extreme poverty
just 20 years ago.

"liberated"? or
confiscated?

Even in this new house, with its
heating and hot water,
my hands are still cold.

How could any hole
in the earth not be cold?
Scissor the clothes, brighten
their color, approximate

some new fashion style:
hat, suit, tie, otherwise
the neck will be cold—
your neck, landlord,
landlady, mine.

Fifth Uncle says,
your great grandpa himself
opened the sheep pan
to the Revolution
waved his hand, OK, he said,
let all be divided up

even their mattress and blankets
were taken from them—

Live on loss
became the family motto
writtenon a scroll on the wall
of the formal sitting room
of the old property.

Fighting the Japanese
your great grandparent's house
was crucial to the underground

for passing food along to the
Anti-Japanese Association.

the day before
the Japanese army attacked
great grandparents opened up
the family larder,

called people from
miles around to come
all that night the farm animals
were agitated. Then at daybreak
all fled into the mountains
The Japanese marching along
the Apricot River
dared not climb the hill.
They got nothing!

That is one part of
our immense pride.

After the war, in the fifties
Some villages revolted against
the landlords,
even killed a few.
But in our village, it was
our great grandpa himself
(he was the village head
for many years)
who called the people
and divide up his own property.

Even today,
Elder Brother says,
our family has many members
many live far away
others come to help,
we of course treat them well:
we don't scrimp on liquor
cigarettes, candy and cookies,
we give many gifts for

a day's labor.

It is soooooo

cooooooooold

but with all of us, somehow, related.
The stoves are more like fire pits,
cooking, setting the table
carrying the coffins,
holding the funeral banners,
wreathes, setting off firecrackers,
filling in the grave

whatever the action / all these
we are reliant on each other
are blessed by, are ensured by
the virtues of the dead.

Cut, cut with scissors, red hat,
yellow boots, sky-blue tie, apricot,
yellow scarves. Only such colors
honor where the ancestors now live
a celestial heavenly palace,
an underground palace . . .

gold mountain,
silver mountain.

Notes: (same as first version; final version
of the poem appears on p. 99.)

ZHANG ER, a poet and opera librettist from Beijing, is the author of multiple books of poetry in Chinese, most recently, *Closest to You,* 离你最近 in 2017. *Verses on Bird* and *So Translating Rivers and Cities* are her previous two bilingual collections in English translation published by Zephyr Press. She also co-edited *Another Kind of Nation: An Anthology of Contemporary Chinese Poetry* published by Talisman House Publishers. Her opera libretti in English include *Moon in the Mirror* (music by Stephen Dembski), which premiered in 2015, and *Fiery Jade: Cai Yan* (music by Gregory Youtz), premiered in 2016.

JOSEPH DONAHUE is an American poet, critic, and editor. He teaches in the English Department of Duke University. Three volumes of an ongoing poetic sequence, *Terra Lucida*, have appeared so far, the most recent, *Dark Church*, in 2015. Other poetry collections include *Incidental Eclipse, Red Flash on a Black Field,* and the forthcoming *Wind Maps.*